The Presence of God

The
Presence
of God

A Supernatural Experience

Ese Duke

ARCHWAY
PUBLISHING

Archway Publishing books may be ordered through booksellers or by contacting:

Archway Publishing
1663 Liberty Drive
Bloomington, IN 47403
www.archwaypublishing.com
844-669-3957

All scripture quotations unless otherwise indicated are taken from the King James Version (KJV) of the Bible

ISBN: 978-1-6657-1309-2 (sc)
ISBN: 978-1-6657-1310-8 (hc)
ISBN: 978-1-6657-1308-5 (e)

Library of Congress Control Number: 2021919911

Print information available on the last page.

Archway Publishing rev. date: 11/11/2021

DEDICATION

First and foremost, I dedicate this book to the precious Holy Spirit, my best friend, senior partner, and guide who has placed a special anointing and imparted His presence upon my life, which has transformed me forever.

I also dedicate this book to the faithful and committed members of Spirit Temple Bible Church Worldwide for their continual support and encouragement in writing this book.

And finally, I dedicate this book to my loving and supportive wife, Reverend Gladys Duke and all my children for their understanding and support of my mandate from God.

CONTENTS

ACKNOWLEDGMENTS

I acknowledge the Father of our Lord Jesus Christ, our King Jesus, and the precious Holy Spirit for the grace to make this book a reality.

Special thanks to all those who contributed their time, resources, and talents to editing and printing this manuscript. Without you, this would not have been a completed masterpiece. May God bless you tremendously and send destiny helpers to every phase of your life's journey. In Jesus' name.

INTRODUCTION

The presence of God is not a theory. It is a reality that once experienced has the ability to transform your life forever. You might be wondering why I am saying this. I have come to understand a lot of people, including Christians, have missed or neglected the act of God's presence because they do not understand what it is or they are not equipped to know what it actually means. Therefore, I found it necessary to discuss the presence of God in this book. As we do so, your life will be radically transformed.

God's presence is different from human presence. God's presence is the atmosphere of heaven and is equal to His person and voice. The more you come to understand the presence of God and how it relates to your life, the more successful your Christian walk will be.

We are about to delve into the discussion of God's presence, through which you will acquire information that will take you to another level in your life, transforming you forever. God's presence is heaven itself. He wants us to experience it on the earth just as Jesus taught His disciples in Matthew 6:10, "Your kingdom come. Your will be done on earth, as it is in heaven." God truly wants us to experience the kingdom atmosphere right here on the earth in our own personal lives.

I pray that as you go through this material, you will understand more about the presence of God, how to apply it, and make it work in your life. There is nothing as tangible and authentic as the presence of God; it is a real experience. When you encounter it based on your knowledge and understanding, your life will never be the same. Your knowledge of God's presence and its application to your life will transform you forever. So let's go on this journey together. Buckle up! It is going to be an exciting ride. You will be extremely glad you have this book in your hand.

CHAPTER ONE

FOUNDATION

Before we delve into the discussion on the presence of God, it is important to receive foundational teaching and an understanding of faith, anointing, and presence.

As said earlier, the presence of God is the atmosphere of heaven. It is the most important phenomenon to experience on planet Earth. As we go deeper into this study, it is essential to lay the right foundation and get a very clear understanding of the meaning of the presence of God. When the foundation is weak, the structure is weak. Therefore, we will first build a strong foundation to help us in our supernatural walk as Christians.

The Christian walk consists of three realms of the supernatural, which are principle, power, and presence (the three Ps):

1. Principle
   This is the realm of faith. Faith is the legal entrance into the realm of the supernatural, and it is the application of the principles of Jesus.

2. Power

   This is the realm of the anointing. The power of the Holy Spirit is what we refer to as the anointing. The anointing is God working through men to do the miraculous.

3. Presence

   This is the realm of glory. The manifest presence of God is when God does what He does without the aid of man. It is initiated by hunger for the glory of the Lord, which originates from God Himself.

Let us look at the differences between these three realms of the supernatural. Knowing the differences is very important. It will help you understand how to operate in them in your supernatural Christian walk.

FAITH

Faith, being the legal entrance into the supernatural, deals more with the basis of the principles of God's Word. In Hebrews 11:6, the Bible says, "Without faith it is impossible to please God, for whoever comes to God must believe that He is the one true God and that He is a rewarder of those who diligently seek Him." The Bible also tells us in Romans 10:17, "Faith comes by hearing and hearing by the Word of God." Even though the faith dimension is the legal entrance to the supernatural, do not let your Christian walk end in this dimension. There is a higher calling.

Faith is the ability given by God to a believer to have dominion over time, space, and matter. In Romans 1:17, the Bible tells us we grow in levels of faith. Your faith can increase as you receive God's Word in your spirit.

Faith is given to you to interrupt the process of time, accelerate the natural, and manifest the supernatural. God's principles will always give you success. Walking by faith will give you success as you apply it to your life, but you do not want to stay there; you want to move your Christian walk to the realm of the anointing.

ANOINTING

The second level of the supernatural is the anointing or the power of God. The anointing is the ability given to the believer by God to do whatever he or she has been called to do. The anointing is Jesus working through humanity. It has to do with divinity at work in and through your humanity. God working through you. The anointing is important, but your Christian walk should not end with the anointing. You should move further to the realm of glory, which is the realm of the presence of God.

GLORY

The third and highest level of the supernatural realm is the glory of God. Glory is the manifest presence of God; this is God's presence manifesting in the physical form. It is God doing His work and operating according to His sovereignty and initiative. In 2 Corinthians 3:18, the Bible tells us we are changed from glory to glory. What can take weeks, months, or even years to accomplish by applying the principle of faith can be accomplished in days or minutes by the anointing. What can take the anointing days, hours, or even minutes to accomplish, can be accomplished instantly by the glory of God. Do not end your Christian walk with faith or the anointing; there is a higher calling. Pursue the glory of God, which is the presence of God.

The glory is the high mark of supernatural living for a child of God. In general, the presence of God can be categorized in three realities:

1. The omnipresence of God (God is everywhere)
2. The indwelling presence of God (God lives in you)
3. The manifest presence of God (God's glory expressed tangibly).

When you have the principle, power, and glory working in your life, you are on your way to experiencing the greatest life ever. Many people just camp around the principle; they do not have the power or the presence.

Some people just camp around the power but do not have the principle or the presence in their lives. Others just camp around the presence of God without the principle of God's Word to guide them or the anointing for the manifestation of the power of God. All three levels of the supernatural should be manifesting in your life. When you manifest these three Ps—the principle, the power, and the presence in your life—things will begin to happen mightily.

Today, most churches all over the world camp around the sermon. Many of them have lost the act of God's presence. What I am about to do is to really get you back into the presence of God and teach you how to manifest His presence in your life. So, open your heart as you read through the pages of this book. You will be saturated in your knowledge and understanding of God's presence so much it will begin to manifest in your life.

THE DIFFERENCE BETWEEN THE ANOINTING AND THE PRESENCE OF GOD

It is very important to understand the difference between the anointing and the presence of God. Knowing the difference will lay the proper foundation as we talk more about the presence of God. Some people think God's presence and the anointing are one and the same, but this is far from the truth.

The presence of God is not the same as the power of God. The other word for God's manifest presence is God's glory. Until you know the difference between the glory and the anointing, you will miss out as a child of God. God wants you not only to walk by faith but to also walk in the anointing and live in His glory. 1 John 2:20–27 tells us as a child of God, you have the unction of the Holy Ghost in you. That is the anointing of God. There is also an anointing that is upon you, which is *dunamis*. That is a Greek word that means "power" from which we get the English word "dynamite." Acts 1:8 says, "Ye shall receive power after the Holy Ghost has come upon you." That power is the anointing, and it is different from the presence. The anointing or power of God will stir you up; it will energize you to perform great wonders. God's presence stills you and makes you want to cry. Isaiah 10:27 says because of the anointing, the yoke shall be taken off your neck and destroyed.

> And it shall come to pass in that day, that his burden shall be taken away from off thy shoulder, and his yoke from off thy neck, and the yoke shall be destroyed because of the anointing. (Isaiah 10:27)

God's anointing upon your life brings about the instant manifestation of dunamis in your life; it is the oil of God that makes your life smooth and easy. In Matthew 11:30, Jesus said,

> For my yoke is easy, and my burden is light. (Matthew 11:30)

God wants His anointing to bring ease into your life. When we talk about the glory of God, it is different from the anointing. The glory of God is the atmosphere of heaven, the atmosphere of God's presence; it is external from us. God's manifest presence is different from God's indwelling presence in your spirit. The manifest presence is the glory realm and it includes angelic hosts. It is the atmosphere where miracles happen.

In the anointing, sickness cannot stand so healing takes place. In the glory, creative miracles take place and sickness is made illegal. When it comes to the anointing, you work. When it comes to the glory, you rest. God's presence brings about rest, while God's anointing puts you to work. You have to function in it.

The anointing of God prepares you for the glory of God (or presence of God) by faith. When it comes to the anointing, the believer takes the initiative through faith, but with the presence of God's glory, God takes the initiative through His sovereignty with the cooperation of the vessel. Faith places a demand on the anointing of an individual. We see this in the story of Elijah and Elisha as recorded in 2 Kings

2:8. Elisha saw Elijah take his mantle and smite the waters, which divided, allowing them to cross over on dry ground. In 2 Kings 2:14, Elisha then put a demand on the anointing that was upon Elijah and did what he observed Elijah do. Calling upon the Lord God of Elijah, Elisha smote the waters, which parted, enabling him to cross over on dry ground. The anointing is God's ability given to a person to fulfill God's purpose, whereas the presence of God is a tangible sovereign manifestation of God's authority. It manifests through His anointed for the purpose of His will and His way to be fulfilled corporately in His time.

In the Old Testament, when the priests ministered and God's presence was heavy, the Bible tells us they were not able to function because of the massive weight of God's glory. God's presence can be a weight that comes upon you that you can hardly stand or be able to function. However, when the anointing is activated by faith, the power of God is manifested.

> So that the priests could not stand to minister by reason of the cloud: for the glory of the LORD had filled the house of God. (2 Chronicles 5:14)

The same testimony is recorded in 1 Kings 8:11:

> So that the priests could not stand to minister because of the cloud: for the glory of the LORD had filled the house of the LORD.

The weight of God's glory on your life melts and calms you; no one can fully stand in His presence. The Bible says the hills melt at the presence of the Lord.

> The hills melted like wax at the presence of the LORD, at the presence of the Lord of the whole earth. (Psalm 97:5)

> The mountains quake at him, and the hills melt, and
> the earth is burned at his presence, yea, the world, and
> all that dwell therein. (Nahum 1:5)

Your life cannot remain the same when God's presence is manifested in it. As we deal with this subject, it is important to get it into your spirit because sooner or later, you will begin to experience the manifestation of God's presence and glory upon your life.

God's power is in God's presence; however, God's power is not the same as God's presence. It is important to note that without the presence of God, there can be no power, for the power (the anointing of God) is released in His presence. The anointing is released more powerfully when you have the awareness of God's presence.

> And his brightness was as the light; he had horns com-
> ing out of his hand: and there was the hiding of his
> power. (Habakkuk 3:4)

Knowing the difference between the anointing (the power) and the presence (the glory), enables you to understand what to do when the anointing and God's presence come upon you. The anointing is God working through you. It stirs you up and you must act by faith to see the power of God manifest or released. On the other hand, the glory stills you; you rest and allow God to do what He needs to do without your effort. So, in the anointing, you act but in the presence, you rest.

For the glory of God to manifest, it must be captured, received, and recognized by our spirits through the revelation of the Holy Ghost. Understanding the difference between glory and the anointing is key to knowing how to cope with the visible manifestation of God's glory in the realm of the natural. One Sunday during service, God's glory was heavy in the house. In my spirit, I heard God say, "Sit down." I sat down right on the stairs of the altar. God's glory manifested heavily and great things began to happen. People were being delivered everywhere as they received a dose of God's presence. Some people were crying and some were on the floor weeping because His glory filled the sanctuary.

Hallelujah! I just sat down and watched what God was doing by His own sovereign act. God's glory is God manifesting by Himself. His power or His anointing is God working in and through you.

As we go into this supernatural experience of the presence of God, I want you to prepare yourself to receive what God has for you. Go past the level of faith and seek the higher call of the anointing. I implore you to even go beyond the anointing to the highest call of glory so you can operate from the realities of the presence of God.

Now that you have this foundational teaching and understanding of faith, anointing, and presence, let us delve into this discussion about the presence of God. Please read on and learn how to pursue the presence of God, enter the presence of God, practice the presence of God, release the presence of God, host the presence of God, cultivate the presence of God, honor the presence of God, celebrate the presence of God, and make room for the presence of God. There is something about the presence of the Lord. When you get to understand all these, it becomes an amazing asset in your life.

CHAPTER TWO

THE PRESENCE
OF GOD

Do you want to experience supernatural provision in your life? If so, it's high time you learn about God's presence so you can experience supernatural provision, supernatural protection, and supernatural providence in your life, just as the Israelites did when they camped around the presence of God.

When you are constantly aware you carry the presence of God, you release and manifest it everywhere you go. Your life changes completely. We must value and recognize the presence of God in our lives, the lives of others, and places where it dwells.

> And what agreement hath the temple of God with idols? for ye are the temple of the living God; as God hath said, I will dwell in them, and walk in them; and I will be their God, and they shall be my people. (2 Corinthians 6:16)

In this scripture, we see it is God's plan and purpose for us to be carriers of His presence. Therefore, we must value it in our lives. We must also understand how to release His presence and let it work in us. God's presence will drive away any demonic activities around you. God's presence will drive away every plan of the Enemy. God's presence will melt every mountain in your life. The principle (the realm of faith) might take some time to bring about manifestation. However, His presence brings about an instant manifestation because in the presence of the Lord is the fullness of joy.

Jesus taught His disciples to pray, "Let your kingdom come." The presence of God is God's kingdom-way of doing things. We can bring about success in our lives and live the kingdom lifestyle by studying and applying the principles of God, which is great. However, Jesus Christ ministered to the people in the presence of God. His principle is what many people turn to when they cannot detect His presence, but God's presence is actually bigger than His principle. The Word of God says the Lord will never leave us; yet, somehow, people still live off the principle. This happens because they have not learned how to discern His presence, so they are forced to live off the principle. Once you understand how to detect the presence of God in your life, how to activate, walk in, and release His presence, you will be so amazed how your life will turn around. The presence of God is the presence of Jesus; it is the presence of the Holy Spirit. The Word of God will draw us to God's presence as we look into it.

The presence of God is not merely a theory; it is a fact and a reality. As God's people, we need to learn about the atmosphere of heaven, which is the presence of God. It is wonderful to have the principle and the anointing, but God's presence needs to be valued and celebrated. In Exodus 33:15, Moses told God, "If your presence will not lead us please do not take us there." Moses knew the importance of the presence of God.

Moses said to God,

I beseech thee, shew me thy glory. (Exodus 33:18)

God then responded to Moses,

> I will make all my goodness pass before thee, and I will
> proclaim the name of the LORD before thee; and will
> be gracious to whom I will be gracious, and will shew
> mercy on whom I will shew mercy. (Exodus 33:19)

Right here, we can see Moses desiring to see God's presence leading him all the days of his journey. The Lord God wants you to appreciate and understand how His presence works. As God's children, we must know we are the temples of the Holy Spirit. Yes, we are the temples of God, and we are to manifest or release the presence of God that is already in us. Throughout this book, whenever I refer to manifesting the presence of God, I am talking about releasing the presence of the Almighty. You will learn how to do that as you read.

In Matthew 6:10, the Lord taught His disciples how to pray. One important phrase in that prayer is, "Thy kingdom come, thy will be done in earth, as it is in heaven." Heaven is filled with the presence of God. The glory of God is the atmosphere of heaven, just for a lack of better words to describe it. The awesomeness of God is released in His presence. The power of God is revealed in His presence. Romans 14:17 says, "God's kingdom is not meat and drink, but it is righteousness, peace and joy in the Holy Ghost." So the kingdom of God is filled with the presence of God. The presence of God is in the power of the Holy Spirit.

When the Word of God becomes spirit (spoken word), the realm of God is released into humanity. In John 6:63, Jesus said, "The words that I speak unto you, they are spirit, and they are life."

> It is the spirit that quickeneth; the flesh profiteth noth-
> ing: the words that I speak unto you, they are spirit, and
> they are life. (John 6:63)

In the realm of God's dominion, God's presence is contained in the realm of the spirit. As we discuss God's presence in this book, there should be a hunger in your spirit to always walk in and release it in your atmosphere, life, and business. God's presence is what you need more than anything else. Once you understand how to release it in your life, it brings peace, joy, provision, and abundance because it can melt every mountain the Enemy brings your way. I know many people have learned a lot about the principles of the Word of God. It is now time to deal with the presence, the glory of God, the *shekinah* glory of God. As you understand more about the shekinah glory of God, your life will be different because you will become a carrier of His presence. You will know how to release, walk, and abide in His presence.

As we deal with this topic, open your heart to the Lord because He really wants you to manifest His presence. It is not only limited to the apostle or a few pastors. It is very important that every child of God walks in His presence. However, it is difficult for you to walk in the presence of God if you do not know or value it. Everything you need is in God's presence. Healing is in His presence. Deliverance is in His presence. Joy, peace, and abundance are in His presence. Learning to live and walk in God's presence propels you quicker to your place of destiny. Think more about the manifest presence of God working in your life. Meditate on the presence of God because God's presence can instantly bring about changes in your life. It can melt every mountain. It can change your circumstances. It can turn a no to a yes. It can open closed doors and do mighty things. When you understand you carry God's presence and learn how to release it, great things will happen in your life.

CHAPTER THREE

THE PURSUIT OF THE PRESENCE OF GOD

The presence of God on your life is the most important phenomenon you can experience. A life without the pursuit of God's presence is a wasted life. People pursue personal dreams; some pursue happiness and others greatness. However, the greatest pursuit of all is the pursuit of the presence of God.

I am not sure where you are in your life, but I believe whatever stage you are at, it is time to have a longing for God. David said,

> As the deer pants for the water brooks, So pants my soul for You, O God. My soul thirsts for God, for the living God. When shall I come and appear before God? (Psalm 42:1–2, NKJV)

One of the obstacles that hinder people from pursuing God or experiencing His presence is problems. This is because their minds drift away from God and focus on the problems. When your mind is focused on God, you will realize the thing you call a big problem is nothing but a mirage. When God's presence consumes your consciousness, the problem becomes small in your reality and fades away as you focus on Him. You become what you focus on, who you look at, or who you think about. When you pursue God, everything else falls into place.

You can only release what is in you and what has consumed you. If you take an orange and squeeze it, orange juice comes out of it, not tomato or pineapple juice. This is because the orange will only produce what is in it naturally. It is filled and concentrated with orange juice.

You release whatever you are consumed with. When you are consumed with problems and afflictions, that is what you release. When you are consumed with God's consciousness, it results in the release of God's presence in your life. I pray you understand how this works and be consumed with God, not afflictions.

The Enemy wants you to think about problems because that distracts you from pursuing God. This is the very thing that happened with David. To maintain his pursuit of God, David had to constantly refocus on Him to remain in the consciousness of His presence.

Apostle Paul said,

> For our light affliction, which is but for a moment,
> worketh for us a far more exceeding and eternal weight
> of glory. (2 Corinthians 4:17)

In this scripture, the phrase "light affliction" might lead you to assume apostle Paul never experienced great turbulence in his journey but that is far from the truth. Apostle Paul went through an enormous ordeal; yet, he referred to his experiences as "light affliction," which means, "a very small problem." You may be wondering, why is that?

Apostle Paul troubled his trouble. It is time for you to make up your mind to trouble your trouble with God's presence. When you trouble your trouble, your trouble stops troubling you. However, when you refuse to trouble your trouble, your trouble will keep troubling you for the rest of your life.

So one may ask, how do you trouble your trouble? You trouble your trouble by making your trouble appear as light affliction, as nothing, as no big deal at all, as apostle Paul did. When you do this, your trouble gets confused, tired, and stops troubling you.

Let's look at the same scripture in the NLT version,

> For our present <u>troubles are small and won't last very long</u>. Yet they produce for us a glory that vastly outweighs them and will last forever! (2 Corinthians 4:17, NLT)

Troubles won't last very long and they are small; yet, they produce glory for us that vastly outweighs them and will last forever. So don't let troubles consume your mind. If you went through trouble about seven years ago, and I ask you to explain the details, you probably would not remember. So don't focus on the trouble.

Let's look at the same scripture in the NIV version,

> For our light and <u>momentary troubles</u> are achieving for us an eternal glory that far outweighs them all. (2 Corinthians 4:17, NIV)

"Momentary trouble" means it is just for a moment.

Are you ready for glory? Are you ready for God's presence? If you are, don't allow the trouble to keep you from pursuing God. Go to God regardless of what you are going through.

Apostle Paul went through a lot of afflictions in life, but he was smart enough to call them light afflictions. Let's look at 2 Corinthians 11:22–33 to see some of the afflictions apostle Paul went through,

> Are they Hebrews? So am I. Are they Israelites? So am I. Are they descendants of Abraham? So am I. Are they servants of Christ? I know I sound like a madman, but I have served him far more! I have worked harder, been put in prison more often, been whipped times without

number, and faced death again and again. Five different times the Jewish leaders gave me thirty-nine lashes. Three times I was beaten with rods. Once I was stoned. Three times I was shipwrecked. Once I spent a whole night and a day adrift at sea. I have traveled on many long journeys. I have faced danger from rivers and from robbers. I have faced danger from my own people, the Jews, as well as from the Gentiles. I have faced danger in the cities, in the deserts, and on the seas. And I have faced danger from men who claim to be believers but are not. I have worked hard and long, enduring many sleepless nights. I have been hungry and thirsty and have often gone without food. I have shivered in the cold, without enough clothing to keep me warm. Then, besides all this, I have the daily burden of my concern for all the churches. Who is weak without my feeling that weakness? Who is led astray, and I do not burn with anger? If I must boast, I would rather boast about the things that show how weak I am. God, the Father of our Lord Jesus, who is worthy of eternal praise, knows I am not lying. When I was in Damascus, the governor under King Aretas kept guards at the city gates to catch me. I had to be lowered in a basket through a window in the city wall to escape from him. (2 Corinthians 11:22–33, NLT)

See what apostle Paul went through? Have you ever had these kinds of problems before? Imagine apostle Paul calling these light afflictions.

If you ever go through problems in your life don't ever say, "I am suffering just like apostle Paul." You are not like apostle Paul. You are not supposed to go through what apostle Paul went through.

Say this out loud, "I will never go through what apostle Paul went through. That is not my portion; it is not my lot. In the name of Jesus!"

Apostle Paul's situation was different, he used to persecute Christians and because of that, Jesus Christ decided he would suffer for Him. This is explained in Acts 9:13–16.

"But Lord," exclaimed Ananias, "I've heard many people talk about the terrible things this man has done to
the believers in Jerusalem! And he is authorized by the
leading priests to arrest everyone who calls upon your
name." But the Lord said, "Go, for Saul is my chosen
instrument to take my message to the Gentiles and to
kings, as well as to the people of Israel. <u>And I will show
him how much he must suffer for my name's sake</u>."
(Acts 9:13–16, NLT)

This happened when Jesus appeared to Ananias and told him He
wanted to send him to Saul. Ananias exclaimed and said, "But Lord,
I've heard many people talk about the terrible things this man has done
to the believers in Jerusalem! And he is authorized by the leading priests
to arrest everyone who calls upon your name." But Jesus said, "Go, for
Saul is my chosen instrument to take my message to the Gentiles, the
kings, as well as the people of Israel." Jesus then said, "I will show him
how much he must suffer for my name's sake." Do you see that? That was
apostle Paul's destiny, not yours. Apostle Paul was mandated to suffer.
So don't say you are supposed to suffer like him.

Say this out loud, "I am not supposed to suffer. I am mandated to
be blessed. God says He has good and wonderful plans for me, a life of
ease. John 10:10 is my portion. In the name of Jesus!"

2 Corinthians 11:22–33 outlines some of the afflictions apostle Paul
went through; and in 2 Corinthians 4:17, apostle Paul referred to these
afflictions as "light affliction." His perspective of these troubles made
all the difference. This helps us understand that the way we see what we
are faced with determines how well we overcome. Apostle Paul saw what
he went through as light affliction and called it just that. This enabled
him to walk over the troubles rather than let them consume his mind
so much they would stop him from pursuing God and fulfilling His
purpose. Apostle Paul troubled his troubles and walked all over them.

Now I want you to shift your mind from the problems and get ready
to pursue God's presence. Don't think about any problems right now,
think about God.

God's presence distinguishes us from unbelievers. Moses said unto God,

> For how then will it be known that Your people and I have found grace in Your sight, except You go with us? So we shall be separate, Your people and I, from all the people who are upon the face of the earth. (Exodus 33:16, NKJV)

Believers should understand as Moses did that the presence of God is what makes us different from other people. Therefore, we should vigorously go after it. However, we must understand the impulse to pursue God's presence comes from God Himself, and we respond to that impulse by following hard, and chasing after Him every time He calls us. We cannot pursue God on our own; He must call us first. The pursuit of God's presence is a call of intimacy with God. Even though His presence is always in us, God calls us to a place where we are intimate with Him. That means, "God puts that urge in us and spurs us to that pursuit." Hence, the Bible tells us,

> No man can come to me, <u>except the Father which hath sent me draw him</u>: and I will raise him up at the last day. (John 6:44)

It is God who puts a hunger in your heart to go after Him. The hunger to pursue God's presence is birthed in you when you let Him know in your heart you need Him more and more. God then calls you to go after Him because He wants you to pursue His presence. He really wants to do something great in your life. Many times, God wants us to go into His presence and He knocks on our doors, but we neglect that call. Do you want to get to a place of higher intimacy with God? If you do, it definitely requires the pursuit of His presence.

One may ask, "Why do we have to pursue or chase after God's presence when indeed, He is the initiator of the whole pursuit?" God takes pleasure when we pursue Him, even though He is the one who gives us the hunger.

> Truly You are a God Who hides Himself, O God of
> Israel, the Savior. (Isaiah 45:15, AMPC)

This scripture tells us God hides Himself, and He wants us to seek and find Him. God wants you to go after Him with all your heart. He wants you to chase after Him. He puts hunger in you to go after His presence because in His presence is fullness of joy; in His presence is peace; in His presence is provision and protection; in His presence is everything you need. The pursuit of His presence originates from God Himself. Your response to that pursuit makes a big difference, and it differentiates you from anybody else who does not know Jesus Christ.

> You will seek me and find me when you seek me with
> all your heart. (Jeremiah 29:13, NIV)

God is not lost, but He wants us to seek Him. Deuteronomy 4:29 tells us when we seek God with all our hearts and souls, we will find Him.

> But if from there you seek the LORD your God, you will
> find him if you seek him with all your heart and with
> all your soul. (Deuteronomy 4:29, NIV)

In this scripture, we see God really wants you to seek Him. He desires you to be in His presence, but He wants you to respond to the hunger He puts in your heart. God puts a hunger in your heart to seek Him and go after His presence because everything you need is in His presence. In Genesis 3:8–11, it is evident from the story of Adam and Eve that God really wants us to seek Him. Even after Adam sinned against God and was running away from Him, God reached out to Adam calling him to His presence.

> And they heard the sound of the Lord God walking in
> the garden in the cool of the day, and <u>Adam and his
> wife hid themselves from the presence of the Lord God</u>
> among the trees of the garden. <u>But the Lord God called</u>

> to Adam and said to him, Where are you? He said, I
> heard the sound of You [walking] in the garden, and I
> was afraid because I was naked; and I hid myself.
>
> And He said, who told you that you were naked? Have
> you eaten of the tree of which I commanded you that
> you should not eat? (Genesis 3:8–11, AMPC)

In this scripture, we see God desires you to seek His presence, not run from it. To the contrary, the Enemy's agenda is to keep you away from God's presence. He wants you to be sin and guilt conscious so you can run away from God's presence. I thank God because Jesus Christ came to take care of the sin problem so you don't have to run away from God's presence. God wants you to chase after Him, not run away from Him. When God is giving you a nudge in your spirit to go after Him, to read your Bible, to pray, to go to church, or to just be alone with Him, it is because He is calling you into His presence. You must answer that call and go after Him with all of your heart. When God calls on you to pursue His presence, your response should be like that of David.

> When You said, "Seek My face," My heart said to You,
> "Your face, LORD, I will seek." (Psalm 27:8, NKJV)

When God calls you into His presence early in the morning, at night, or whatever time, your heart should respond as David's heart did, saying, "Your face, LORD, will I seek." God truly wants every one of His children to desire His presence, seek His presence, and go after Him. The greatest pursuit in your life should be the pursuit of God's presence, not the pursuit of money, fame, greatness, or any other feat. When your greatest pursuit in life is the pursuit of God's presence, life becomes more meaningful, enjoyable, and purposeful. God's presence gives you everything you need because you cannot be in it and experience defeat. You cannot be in God's presence and experience lack. You cannot be in His presence and experience calamity in your life. In God's presence, everything He Has purposed begins to work out for you. Every child of God should desire God's presence as the psalmist did in Psalm 42:1–2,

> As the hart panteth after the water brooks, so panteth my soul after thee, O God. My soul thirsteth for God, for the living God: when shall I come and appear before God? (Psalm 42:1–2)

David was going hard after God. Thus, in Acts 13:22, God called him a man after His own heart.

> And when he had removed him, he raised up unto them David to be their king; to whom also he gave their testimony, and said, <u>I have found David</u> the son of Jesse, <u>a man after mine own heart</u>, which shall fulfill all my will. (Acts 13:22)

David desired to be in God's presence, so he started seeking and chasing after God. Your soul should long after God as David's soul did: in your prayer life, in your study life, and in your meditation. Let God's presence be the most important thing in your life, and let everything you do be about it. You might ask; why is the pursuit of the presence of God so important? David said:

> How lovely is your dwelling place, O Lord of Heaven's Armies. (Psalm 84:1, NLT)

David understood the importance of being in God's presence. I know God's presence is within you, but God wants you to pursue His face, His person, His voice, and His presence. David proceeded to say,

> I long, yes, I faint with longing to enter the courts of the Lord. With my whole being, body and soul, I will shout joyfully to the living God. (Psalm 84:2, NLT)

When was the last time you had a strong desire to always be in the house of God? When was the last time you could not wait for the church doors to open? David was a man after God's own heart, and he talked about how lovely God's dwelling place is. I understand God lives in us, but we go to a place where we know His presence is always manifesting. David said, "I long, yes, I faint with longing to enter the courts of the LORD." In verse 4 of the same scripture, the Bible goes on to tell us,

> What joy for those who can live in your house, always
> singing your praises. (Psalm 84:4, NLT)

Your eagerness to be in the house of the Lord is an indication of your pursuit of His presence. When all your plans, purposes, and the agenda of your life are centered on God and His place of worship, this is an indication you are pursuing God's presence. When you are in pursuit of God's presence, great things begin to happen in your life. Psalm 22:3 says God inhabits the praises of His people. This means His presence is evident in the praises of His people.

Matthew 18:20 tells us where two or three are gathered in His name, He is there in their midst. Therefore, Hebrews 10:25 admonishes us not to neglect the assembling of ourselves together. The admonition is given because some people have the habit of not coming together as a body of believers in the church. When we come together as believers, Jesus promises to be right there in our midst. Pursuing God's presence is not just in our prayer life, but it is also in our assembling together as believers and our praises to Him.

Your eagerness to put God first in your life, thoughts, actions, and walk, as well as planning your life around the things of God, the house of God, and the ways of God, is an indication of your pursuit of God's presence in you. It also indicates to God where your heart is. As we pursue God's presence, we should remember it is evident in the temple and gathering of His people. No wonder David said he looked for God in the sanctuary to see His power and glory.

> O God, You are my God; Early will I seek You; My
> soul thirsts for You; My flesh longs for You In a dry and

thirsty land Where there is no water. So <u>I have looked</u> <u>for You in the sanctuary, To see Your power and Your</u> <u>glory</u>. (Psalm 63:1–2, NKJV)

Why did David pursue the presence of God? The answer is in Psalm 63:3–8.

Because Your lovingkindness is better than life, My lips shall praise You. Thus I will bless You while I live; I will lift up my hands in Your name.

My soul shall be satisfied as with marrow and fatness,

And my mouth shall praise You with joyful lips.

When I remember You on my bed, I meditate on You in the night watches.

Because You have been my help, Therefore in the shadow of Your wings I will rejoice.

My soul follows close behind You; Your right hand up- holds me. (Psalm 63:3–8, NKJV)

In this scripture, David the psalmist, a man after God's own heart, is giving us the nugget of truth about how to pursue God's presence. David could not wait to be in the house of the Lord. He could not wait to seek God early in the morning, right on his bed while he was lying down, meditating on Him in the night watches. David was always thinking about God, pursuing God, and going hard after God; his soul longed for God. Let your pursuit of God's presence be lifelong because in His presence, there is fulfillment for living and joy for existence.

Don't let your life be only about going after the things of this world; let it be about going after the things of God, for the Bible tells us,

But seek ye first the kingdom of God, and his righteousness; and all these things shall be added unto you. (Matthew 6:33)

When God puts a hunger in you to go after Him, do that, because God really wants you to walk and live in His presence. When you live your life in God's presence, you are living it just as Jesus Christ did. Jesus lived in God's presence.

Most people today live their lives on the principle of Jesus but when you live in His presence, it is the greatest thing ever. To live in God's presence requires going hard after Him. Pursuing God's presence is making sure early in the morning, you desire Him. In the night watches, God should always be on your mind. You should go hard after Him and not allow anything that would make Him secondary in your life take your attention. When you let God come first in your life, your pursuit of His presence will bring you promotion and divine provision. Your pursuit of God's presence will also lead you to a place of greatness and prominence. I challenge you, make the pursuit of God's presence your greatest priority in life, and you will see how God moves in and through you beyond your wildest dreams. Pursue His presence and enjoy a fulfilled life.

CHAPTER FOUR

ENTERING THE PRESENCE OF GOD

———

What does it mean to enter the presence of God? How can you and I enter the presence of the Lord all the time?

As New Testament believers, it is important to understand the presence and glory of God reside inside of us. In the Old Testament, God's presence and glory were outside of those who believed in God.

> And David gathered all Israel together to Jerusalem, to bring up the ark of the LORD unto his place, <u>which he had prepared for it</u>. (1 Chronicles 15:3)

The ark represents the presence of God. From this scripture, we can see David prepared an external place for it.

> And said unto them, Ye are the chief of the fathers of the Levites: <u>sanctify yourselves</u>, both ye and your brethren,

that ye may bring up the ark of the LORD God of Israel
unto the <u>place that I have prepared for it</u>. For because ye
did it not at the first, the LORD our God made a breach
upon us, for that we <u>sought him not after the due order</u>.
(1 Chronicles 15:12–13)

Note that the priests of the Levites sanctified themselves to bring up
the ark of the Lord God of Israel. I want you to take note of the following
in the preceding scripture:

1. The ark represents the presence of God and entering God's
   presence requires due order.
2. David gathered all the Israelites together to prepare themselves
   to enter God's presence.

Psalm 16:11 tells us in the presence of God there is fullness of joy
and pleasures for evermore.

Thou wilt shew me the path of life: in thy presence is
fulness of joy; at thy right hand there are pleasures for
evermore. (Psalm 16:11)

In God's presence there is rest, peace, liberty, joy, and content-
ment. Every child of God must practice entering God's presence all
the time. It is important to note that anyone can enter the presence
of God. As New Testament believers, God is in us; His presence is
not outside of us. This brings us back to our question, "What does
it really mean to enter God's presence, and how can we enter God's
presence?" David said,

Whither shall I go from thy spirit? or whither shall I flee
from thy presence?

If I ascend up into heaven, thou art there: if I make my
bed in hell, behold, thou art there. (Psalm 139:7–8)

In this scripture, we see there is no place we can go that God is not already there; God's presence is with us. So, since we understand God is everywhere, we now know we are the ones who have a problem experiencing Him and feeling His presence, which is very near us. Entering God's presence means being aware of the reality of His presence in our lives. To enter the presence of God is to experience the reality of the Holy Spirit; it does not mean to go somewhere. It means to become aware and conscious of what is true; God is with you. To experience God or feel His presence, we must train our spirits and souls to become aware of the Holy Spirit.

Let's take a close look at Hebrews 10:19,

> Having therefore, brethren, boldness to enter into the holiest by the blood of Jesus.

In this scripture, to "enter" means "to draw near, to approach, to go into, or to access the presence of God." You can train yourself to become aware of the Holy Spirit. You become aware of people when you can hear, see, and feel them. In the same way, you become aware of God when you position yourself to hear, see, and feel Him.

During worship service, people tend to think of doing two things:

1. Trying to bring God down
2. Trying to get into some place where God is

These are wrong concepts that cause you to strive and stress out. Worship service is basically becoming aware of what is always true: God is with us. Once you understand how to enter God's presence all the time, you will realize the things that used to be difficult in your life become easy. The Bible says in God's presence every mountain melts. In His presence every difficulty disappears. In His presence there is peace, love, and joy. When you enter His presence, you will experience your best life ever.

> That they should seek the Lord, if haply they might feel after him, and find him, though he be not far from

> every one of us, For <u>in him we live</u>, and <u>move</u>, and <u>have our being</u>; as certain also of your own poets have said, For we are also his offspring. (Acts 17:27–28)

In this scripture, we can see it is in God we live, and the Spirit of God resides inside of us. Back in the Old Testament, His presence was outside. They had to carry the Ark of the Covenant to represent His presence. The Bible tells us we are the temples of God.

> And what agreement hath the temple of God with idols? For <u>ye are the temple of the living God</u>; as God hath said, <u>I will dwell in them</u>, and <u>walk in them</u>; and I will be their God, and they shall be my people. (2 Corinthians 6:16)

We can see God's presence is in us. The reality of that fact alone will help us enter His presence that resides inside us.

When I talk about entering God's presence, I am referring to realizing, perceiving, and becoming conscious of His presence. This happened in the book of Genesis,

> And Jacob awaked out of his sleep, and he said, surely the LORD is in this place; and I knew it not. (Genesis 28:16)

In this scripture, we see prior to Jacob's awakening from his sleep, he was not aware of God's presence. He was not conscious of it so he did not know the Lord was in that place. There are various ways to realize God's presence in your life. God reveals Himself to those who seek Him earnestly. You must desire and hunger to be in God's presence and be more aware of it. The presence of God must be a priority in the life of His people.

David said,

> As the hart panteth after the water brooks, so panteth my soul after thee, O God. My soul thirsteth for God,

for the living God: when shall I come and appear before
God? (Psalm 42:1–2)

Interestingly, this was David's prayer, he desired to be in God's presence. However, as a New Testament Christian, you carry His presence. Your awareness of God's presence in your life is what gets you to enter His presence. You must know you have His presence in your life and be consciously aware of it. Even Moses told us,

> Now therefore, I pray thee, if I have found grace in thy sight, shew me now thy way, that I may know thee, that I may find grace in thy sight: and consider that this nation is thy people. And he said, My presence shall go with thee, and I will give thee rest. And he said unto him, If thy presence go not with me, carry us not up hence. (Exodus 33:13–15)

1 Chronicles 15:12–13 says you must prepare your heart before God. That means to prepare the temple before God comes. So, in the practice of entering God's presence, you must first prepare your heart. You must have a heart of love for God. You must love God with all of your heart, soul, and mind (Matthew 22:37). You have to put God first in your life by loving Him more than anything or anyone else. As you do this, entering His presence becomes easy. It is through your love for God, which is demonstrated by you seeking Him that prepares your heart to be in His presence.

Preparing your heart to enter God's presence will require thanksgiving, praise, and worship. In Psalm 100:4, David said, "Enter into His gates with thanksgiving and into His courts with praise. Be thankful unto him, and bless his name." Thanksgiving and praise are utterances, but worship is an attitude. God wants you to make utterances of thanksgiving, praise, and have an attitude of worship. The Bible tells us thanksgiving relates to God's goodness (Psalm 118:1); praise relates to God's greatness (Psalm 145:3), and worship relates to God's holiness (Psalm 29:2). As you give God thanks for His goodness, praise His holy name for His greatness, and worship Him for the beauty of His holiness, His presence will manifest in your life. Entering His presence becomes very easy in your life. To experience entering God's presence all the time, you must be aware of His presence in your life continually.

> Serve the LORD with gladness: come before his presence with singing. Know ye that the LORD he is God: it is he that hath made us, and not we ourselves; we are his people, and the sheep of his pasture. Enter into his gates with thanksgiving, and into his courts with praise: be thankful unto him, and bless his name.
>
> For the LORD is good; his mercy is everlasting; and his truth endureth to all generations. (Psalm 100:2–5)

From the scripture, we see that there are various steps to entering God's presence. Realistically, entering God's presence is the awareness of it in your life, which is brought about through thanksgiving, praise, and worship. Thanksgiving unto God will take you into His gates; praise will take you into His courts; and worship will take you directly into the presence of the Holy Spirit. To enter God's presence you must have a lifestyle of worship, not just thanksgiving and praise. You have to worship the Lord with all your heart. If you do not have a lifestyle of worship, you cannot be aware of God's presence all the time. God wants to release His power in your life, and His power can only be released in His presence. As you begin to worship the Lord, desiring a fresh experience with Him every morning and constantly being aware of His presence, you will begin to understand that entering His presence is very easy.

It is important to understand that as a New Testament believer, you are not trying to enter His presence outside of you, but His presence in you. God wants you to enter His presence today. In other words, God wants you to have the awareness of His presence in your life today. The only way to enter the presence of God is through a lifestyle of thanksgiving, praise, and worship. Why don't you try that today? When worship becomes your lifestyle, you will begin to experience God's presence in an even greater dimension. As you are saturated with God's presence, you can do great things for His kingdom because you live your life in His presence.

Living your life from the presence of God comes as a result of your constant awareness of His presence, which enables you to be in it all the time. Remember, His presence is not outside of you; it is within you, and your awareness of His presence gets you into His presence all the time. You are not trying to enter; you are in it by your awareness of it. Your consciousness and perception of God's presence in your spirit equals to entering His presence. Do not continue to act like those who do not know or understand the presence of God. You should now have a new level of consciousness that His presence lives in you, and as long as you are aware of it, you are always in it. You don't have to try to enter in next week; you are always in His presence. Being consciously aware of His presence all the time makes the difference.

You are not like David in the Old Testament who cried out to God in Psalm 51:11 saying, "Cast me not away from thy presence; and take not thy Holy Spirit from me." You are a carrier of God's presence, and He will not take the Holy Spirit from you. He promised in Hebrews 13:5 never to leave you or forsake you. Also, Jesus told the disciples,

> And I will ask the Father, and He will give you another Helper (Comforter, Advocate, Intercessor—Counselor, Strengthener, Standby), to be with you forever— the Spirit of Truth, whom the world cannot receive [and take to its heart] because it does not see Him or know Him, but you know Him because He (the Holy Spirit) remains with you continually and will be in you. (John 14:16–17, AMP)

In this scripture, we see the Holy Spirit will be with you forever. He remains with you continually and will be in you. David, an Old Testament believer said, "Cast me not away from thy presence and take not thy Holy Spirit from me" because the Holy Spirit came upon the Old Testament believers when they had to be used by God. As a New Testament believer, the Holy Spirit dwells in you. Since God's presence is already inside you, all you must do to enter is be aware it is in your life. When you live like that, think like that, and act like that, you will see God manifesting greatly in you.

Now, having acquired this knowledge let me share with you some practical ways to apply it and enter or experience the presence of God.

KEYS TO EXPERIENCING THE PRESENCE OF THE HOLY SPIRIT

1. Gratitude/Thanksgiving
    Always be thankful and appreciate God for what He has done. The opposite of this would be complaining, being negative, critical, and ungrateful.

    > I will praise the name of God with a song, and will magnify him with thanksgiving. (Psalm 69:30)

2. Praise
    Focus your attention on God by acknowledging what He has done.

    > Enter into his gates with thanksgiving, and into his courts with praise: be thankful unto him, and bless his name. (Psalm 100:4)

    > By him therefore let us offer the sacrifice of praise to God continually, that is, the fruit of our lips giving thanks to his name. (Hebrews 13:15)

3. Worship
    Worship is the expression of true respect or reverence for God. It is a function of the heart that pleases God.

    > Therefore, since we are receiving a kingdom that can- not be shaken, let us be thankful, and so worship

God acceptably with reverence and awe, (Hebrews 12:28, NIV)

The same scripture in the NLT rendering says,

> Since we are receiving a Kingdom that is unshakable, let us be thankful and please God by worshiping him with holy fear and awe. (Hebrews 12:28, NLT)

What makes you a worshipper is not your ability to sing worship songs but your ability to live conscious of God daily, connecting to Him spirit to spirit. Whatever you worship possesses you.

> Yet a time is coming and has now come when the true worshipers will worship the Father in the Spirit and in truth, for they are the kind of worshipers the Father seeks. God is spirit, and his worshipers must worship in the Spirit and in truth. (John 4:23–24, NIV)

4. Meditation
   Fix your mind on Him. Focus on Him. Think of Him.

> Set your affection on things above, not on things on the earth. (Colossians 3:2)

This scripture tells us to set our minds on the things that are above.

> I have set the Lord always before me: because he is at my right hand, I shall not be moved. (Psalm 16:8)

Meditation is using your imagination to fix your focus or mind on the truth. You can imagine the truth, and begin to determine what it looks like and what it feels like. As you continue to do this, your heart opens up to where your mind goes.

5. Confidence
   Confidence is based on knowing and holding on to what the Word of God says about us.

   > Let us therefore come boldly unto the throne of grace, that we may obtain mercy, and find grace to help in time of need. (Hebrews 4:16)

   > There is therefore now no condemnation to them which are in Christ Jesus, who walk not after the flesh, but after the Spirit. (Romans 8:1)

   You must resist and overcome negative and condemning thoughts in order to increase your confidence.

6. Expectation
   Don't be passive; expect the Holy Spirit to respond. To expect is to anticipate and look for the experience of His presence. His presence is real. You can see, hear, and feel the presence of God.

   > I was in the Spirit on the Lord's day, and heard behind me a great voice, as of a trumpet. (Revelation 1:10)

7. Focus
   Focus means, "to eliminate distractions and give your attention to one thing." Tune into impressions and watch for the sensations in your heart. As you focus on and continue doing this, watch for His presence. You will see, hear, and feel it.

   > Then as I looked, I saw a door standing open in heaven, and the same voice I had heard before spoke to me like a trumpet blast. The voice said, "Come up here, and I will show you what must happen after this." (Revelation 4:1, NLT)

8. Waiting

    Waiting is not being passive; it is resting in the love of God in anticipation of intimacy.

    > Wait on the Lord: be of good courage, and he shall strengthen thine heart: wait, I say, on the Lord. (Psalm 27:14)

9. Respond to the Holy Spirit's Impressions

    As you sense the prompting presence of the Holy Spirit, respond by pursuing Him more and act upon what you receive.

    > And he said unto them, Take heed what ye hear: with what measure ye mete, it shall be measured to you: and unto you that hear shall more be given. (Mark 4:24)

    In this scripture we see that, to him who hears, more shall be given.

10. Yielding

    Yielding is intentionally responding to the impressions and leading of the Holy Spirit.

    > And said, "Assuredly, I say to you, unless you are converted and become as little children, you will by no means enter the kingdom of heaven. (Matthew 18:3, NKJV)

    Yielding is being childlike. Children are trusting and responsive to adults.

11. Sensitivity

    Don't grieve the Holy Spirit. Identify attitudes and actions that grieve Him and quickly address them by repentance, which means, "a change of mind." We grieve the Holy Spirit by the words we speak and the condition of our hearts. Pay close attention to the words you speak and your heart's condition. When you do, you will experience the manifest presence of God.

> Let him that stole steal no more: but rather let him labour, working with his hands the thing which is good, that he may have to give to him that needeth.

> Let no corrupt communication proceed out of your mouth, but that which is good to the use of edifying, that it may minister grace unto the hearers.

> And grieve not the Holy Spirit of God, whereby ye are sealed unto the day of redemption. (Ephesians 4:28–30)

12. Practice His Presence
    Develop a lifestyle that tunes into and responds to the Holy Spirit.

> Pray without ceasing. (1 Thessalonians 5:17)

CHAPTER FIVE

PRACTICING THE PRESENCE OF GOD

After knowing how to enter God's presence, it's important to now talk about how to practice that presence. To better understand how to engage the realm of the spirit, preliminary groundwork must be laid. With this in place, we can practice the presence of God to produce results at all times. Let's look at Exodus 33:16, NLT version:

> How will anyone know that you look favorably on me—
> on me and on your people—if you don't go with us? For
> your presence among us sets your people and me apart
> from all other people on the earth.

The manifest presence of God upon our lives is the distinguishing factor between us, God's people, and the other people on the earth. People may live good lives and have good things in life. In as much as God blesses us with all of that, what makes a child of God distinct from a nonbeliever is the abiding manifest presence of God. It is not just prosperity or the life of ease they enjoy.

It's important to note when Jesus walked on this earth, He was constantly aware of the presence of the Holy Spirit and the Father. He knew He was never alone.

> Behold, the hour cometh, yea, is now come, that ye shall be scattered, every man to his own, and shall leave me alone: and yet I am not alone, because the Father is with me. (John 16:32)

We must learn how to become conscious and aware of God's presence, which comes as we understand what practicing it actually means and applying what we learn. We must cultivate an intimate fellowship with God through the Holy Spirit.

When we talk about practicing God's presence, it is important to note it is a supernatural encounter, and everything that has to do with the supernatural begins with faith. You must come to the realization faith connects you to the Spirit and the supernatural realm of God. Let me give you a few examples to drive this point home. Let's look at the story of the woman with the issue of blood in Matthew 9:21–22,

> For she said within herself, If I may but touch his garment, I shall be whole. But Jesus turned him about, and when he saw her, he said, Daughter, be of good comfort; thy faith hath made thee whole. And the woman was made whole from that hour. (Matthew 9:21–22)

The phrase, "she said within herself" in Matthew 9:21 means, she was constantly thinking and speaking to herself. She said, if she could only touch the hem of His garment, she would be made whole. She was imagining within herself. That is a form of meditation. When we look at verse 22 of the same scripture, we notice her faith connected her to the supernatural realm based on her belief, which is evident in what she said to herself and what she was constantly thinking.

Let's look at the story of the man with a son tormented with demonic spirits in Mark 9:21–24 for another example of how faith connects us to the Spirit and the supernatural realm of God.

> And he asked his father, How long is it ago since this came unto him? And he said, Of a child.
>
> And ofttimes it hath cast him into the fire, and into the waters, to destroy him: but if thou canst do anything, have compassion on us, and help us.
>
> Jesus said unto him, <u>If thou canst believe, all things are possible to him that believeth</u>. And straightway the father of the child cried out, and said with tears, Lord, I believe; help thou mine unbelief. (Mark 9:21–24)

Here we see how faith was required to connect to the supernatural realm of possibilities for the miraculous. In verse 23, Jesus said, "If you can believe, all things are possible to him that believes." The key and primary ingredient to obtaining a miracle in the realm of the spirit or the supernatural is faith. Faith connects you to the supernatural realm of possibilities. So practicing the presence of God requires faith, which is a deep conviction and belief in your heart.

In 2 Corinthians 5:7, the Bible tells us, "We walk by faith, not by sight." We need to focus on what God says and His ability and be indifferent (pay no attention) to what we see in the physical.

There are two realms of the mind: the natural realm and the spirit realm. Walking by sight refers to walking by your senses; this occurs in the natural realm of the mind where you only see with your optical eyes. Walking by faith refers to perceiving as real what is not yet revealed to the senses. It is revealed in the Word of God as a reality. This occurs in the spirit realm of the mind where you see through the eyes of the spirit (faith). Faith is a product of the recreated spirit; it only sees what God says as revealed in His Word. Many times, we neglect the feeling part of the faith dimension, but in Hebrews 11:1, it is clearly stated that faith has to do with perception and a feeling in our hearts.

> Now faith is the assurance (the confirmation, the title deed) of the things [we] hope for, being the proof of things [we] do not see and the conviction of their reality [faith perceiving as real fact what is not revealed to the senses]. (Hebrews 11:1, AMPC)

We experience what we are thinking in our hearts; we actually feel our thoughts. Until you understand this aspect of faith (which is a product of your heart; that is, your recreated spirit), you may not be able to experience the presence to the dimension God desires His children to. People do not experience the tangible presence of God because they lack understanding. When practicing God's presence, we must learn how to open our hearts, our inner man or spirit, and connect our thoughts and feelings to our hearts. We can actually experience and feel His presence around us, within us, and in our hearts. That means we must exercise our senses to develop our spiritual awareness, consciousness, and feelings. Most people know, or have learnt, how to shut down, or block their feelings from what they do not desire in their lives. They decide where to open their feelings to. In the same way, we can open our hearts, our inner man, or spirits, to connect to our thoughts and feelings.

Imagination connects us to the realm of the spirit. Imagination is in the realm of the unseen in the material world but can be seen in the immaterial world. Imagination is a gift from God that we have as children. Most people discard it as they get older because it does not make material sense to them. If it makes sense, it is in the material world and the material world is of the natural. If it does not make sense due to the fact that it is not seen yet, it exists in the immaterial world. This is so because in the realm of the spirit, everything is ready; everything is given, and everything is possible.

You can use your imagination to get into the reality of availability and all possibilities. It is through imagination that people make the impossible become possible. Imagination is a mental picture in the realm of the spirit. It is more like a virtual world you see with the eyes of the spirit or of your heart. It talks to you and connects you to the realm of the spirit. It's an act of picturing situations or conversations that have not yet taken place or occurred. Imagination is in the realm of the spirit and with it comes a lot of possibilities. All creation comes from this realm. Think of God saying, "It's not good for man to be alone, I will make him a helper suitable for him" (Genesis 2:18). Out of that imagination God had, the woman was created for Adam.

The spirit realm consists of the Spirit of God and demonic spirits as well, so the realm of the spirit has to be entered with proper understanding. Therefore, learning to practice the presence of God becomes a safeguard to a child of God as we walk by faith in the spirit/supernatural realm.

There are two ways to connect to the spirit world: vain imaginations and meditation. Vain imaginations connect you to demonic spirits. On the contrary, meditating on the truth of God's Word connects you to God.

Let's talk about vain imaginations. In Exodus 20:4 the Bible says,

> Thou shalt not make unto thee any graven image, or any likeness of anything that is in heaven above, or that is in the earth beneath, or that is in the water under the earth.

In this instance, man, through vain imagination, creates an idol or graven image, which connects him to the demonic spirit that is behind the graven image.

> Then the Lord said to me: "Son of dust, have you seen what the elders of Israel are doing in their minds? For they say, 'The Lord doesn't see us; he has gone away!'" (Ezekiel 8:12, TLB)

The elders of Israel created demonic imagery in their minds. Vain imaginations connect you to the demonic spirits behind the images created in the mind.

Let's take a look at the King James Version of the same scripture:

> Then said he unto me, Son of man, hast thou seen what the
> ancients of the house of Israel do in the dark, every man in
> the <u>chambers of his imagery</u>? For they say, the LORD seeth
> us not; the LORD hath forsaken the earth. (Ezekiel 8:12)

"Chambers of imagery" refer to the inner man, or a concealed private room, where the imagination of vanity occurs. A spirit is at work behind every imagination. Imaginations are in the unseen world, so it is a function of the human spirit to call or connect to the demonic spirits or the Spirit of God. As the Scripture says, "The deep calls unto deep" (Psalm 42:7). If a conversation is imagined and fear is involved, most likely a picture is in your mind, which affects your feelings. That imagery is induced by the spirit of fear.

When people watch pornography, there is a picture in their minds that produces a feeling, which is induced by the spirit of perversion. In video gaming that involves sorcery or witchcraft, there is a picture in the mind, which produces a feeling induced by the spirit of witchcraft or sorcery. Imagination definitely connects you to the realm of the spirit, and meditating on the truth of God's Word connects you to God. This is the place of deep intimacy with almighty God, where deep calls unto deep and spirit calls unto spirit.

Spirit calling unto spirit is in the world of deep meditation and imagination, which involves your heart until you are consumed with your imagination that lines up with the Word of God. That kind of fellowship or intimacy of the deep, and consummation of the deep calling unto deep, is only found in the realm of the spirit. The imagination engages the feelings and the spirit world behind the thought. To meditate is to engage the imagination to picture and feel thoughts.

> I call to remembrance my song in the night; <u>I meditate</u>
> <u>within my heart</u>, And <u>my spirit makes diligent search</u>.
> (Psalm 77:6, NKJV)

This scripture says, "I meditate within my heart; my spirit makes diligent search." There is a connection between meditation and the activity of the inner man or the spirit man to reach out to God.

You use your imagination to see and feel thoughts. For example, when you think the following thoughts, you feel what you are thinking: the love of God, the joy of the LORD, the compassion of God, the peace of God, the glory of God, the anointing, the forgiveness of God, and then, the presence of God!

BASIC KEYS TO PRACTICING THE PRESENCE OF GOD

1. You Must Free and Open up Your Spirit.
   This can be done effectively by praying in the spirit, which energizes your spirit man to engage God in the realm of the Spirit.

2. There Must Be Faith and Expectation
   Faith and expectation are necessary to experience or have an encounter with the presence of God. James 4:8a says, "Draw nigh to God and He will draw nigh to you." This is done in your consciousness and imagination, which is the faculty of the spirit (heart).

3. Focus Your Thoughts, Imagination, and Mind
   You have to focus your thoughts, imagination, and mind (soul) toward the truth: the presence of God. You must picture it clearly in your imagination.

4. Use Your Imagination
   You have to use your imagination to engage the truth of God's presence in your inner man. Frequently repeat this process until you establish a pathway to encounter the presence of God.

5. Spend Time With God
   Spending each day and time alone with God, thanking Him, praising Him, worshiping Him, and having the consciousness of His presence throughout the day will help you to practice His presence in your life.

CHAPTER SIX

RELEASING THE PRESENCE OF GOD

This subject is very important and dear to my heart because it is in God's presence our miracles are birthed. The presence of God is contained in the realm of the Spirit, which is the realm of God's dominion. If you say what the Father says, you begin to operate in the realm of the Spirit.

We cannot talk about the presence of God without talking about the person of the Holy Spirit. The secret to releasing God's presence is in the person of the Holy Spirit; therefore, understanding who the person of the Holy Spirit is will help us release God's presence in our lives. To release the presence of God it is important to acquire knowledge in the following areas:

1. The person of the Holy Spirit
2. Talking to the Holy Spirit
3. Meditating on the Holy Spirit
4. Being aware of the Holy Spirit

Releasing the presence of God is very important to every child of God. Until you learn to release the presence of God, you will not be able to fulfill your destiny in Him. Learning these secrets will help you to release God's presence.

SECRETS TO RELEASING THE PRESENCE OF GOD

1. The Person of the Holy Spirit
   The Holy Spirit, the very breath of God, the *ruach* (a Hebrew word that means "breath") of God is a person. He is not a force, and He is not fire. Once you know Him as a person, it makes a great difference in your life.

   > And I will ask the Father, and He will give you another Helper (Comforter, Advocate, Intercessor—Counselor, Strengthener, Standby), to be with you forever— the Spirit of Truth, whom the world cannot receive [and take to its heart] because it does not see Him or know Him, but you know Him because He (the Holy Spirit) remains with you continually and will be in you. (John 14:16–17, AMP)

   In this scripture, we see Jesus Christ speaking to His disciples telling them about the Holy Spirit, the Comforter. Jesus Christ called the Holy Spirit an advocate and in 1 John 2:1, we see Jesus Christ is also said to be our advocate.

   > My little children, these things write I unto you, that ye sin not. And if any man sin, we have an advocate with the Father, Jesus Christ the righteous. (1 John 2:1)

   The Holy Spirit is a person just like Jesus, and He proceeds from the Father. Jesus Christ said,

> But when the Comforter is come, whom I will send
> unto you from the Father, even the Spirit of truth, which
> proceedeth from the Father, he shall testify of me: (John
> 15:26)

I want you to be very attentive to what I am sharing with you about the Holy Spirit; your understanding of this will help you release His presence wherever you go. You cannot talk about releasing the presence of God without understanding the person of the Holy Spirit. The Bible says Christ designated the Holy Spirit as a paraclete. In John 14:16, Jesus calls the Holy Spirit *Allos Parakletos*. Allos is a Greek word that means, "another of equal quality," not *Heteros*, which means, "another of different quality." Parakletos is a Greek word that means, "comforter" or "advocate." Therefore, the Holy Spirit is described by Jesus Christ as equal with Himself and equal with God.

> And I will pray the Father, and he shall give you another
> Comforter, that he may abide with you forever; (John
> 14:16)

The Holy Spirit is called a paraclete because He is another one just like Jesus, and He undertakes Christ's office in the world while Christ is away from the world as the God-man. So, it is important to understand the Holy Spirit is a person. With this understanding, you will be able to release the presence of God into any situation in your life, and when you do, you will experience tremendous victory. However, if you don't know the person of the Holy Spirit, it is difficult to release His presence subconsciously wherever you are.

> For His divine power has bestowed upon us all things
> that [are requisite and suited] to life and godliness,
> through the [full, personal] knowledge of Him Who
> called us by and to His own glory and excellence (virtue).
> By means of these He has bestowed on us His precious

and exceedingly great promises, so that through them you may escape [by flight] from the moral decay (rottenness and corruption) that is in the world because of covetousness (lust and greed), and become sharers (partakers) of the divine nature. (2 Peter 1:3–4, AMPC)

This scripture tells us we are partakers of His divine nature; we have divinity in our humanity. To be able to release His presence, you must understand the Holy Spirit is a person and He resides in you. Therefore, you are a partaker of the divinity by the means of the person of the Holy Spirit. It is God's plan and purpose for you to release His presence wherever you are.

2. Talking to the Holy Spirit
    The Holy Spirit is a person; talking to Him is as simple as speaking to a friend. You can speak to Him, ask Him a question, and wait for an answer. Talking to Him means you have an awareness of His presence with you. Don't leave your bed without saying good morning to the Holy Spirit.

3. Meditating on the Holy Spirit
    To meditate means, "To think on." Think on the Holy Spirit. Think about His love, provision, peace, and all He brings into your life. Just think about Him the same way you think about Jesus. He is a person, not a dove. Have the right thoughts about Him.

4. Being Aware of the Holy Spirit
    You must be aware the Holy Spirit resides in you and be conscious of His presence. The awareness of His presence should be a part of your everyday life.

    God wants you to release His presence everywhere you are but you must know the Holy Spirit as a person. You must talk to the Holy Spirit all the time. You must think about the Holy Spirit and be aware of His presence.

WHAT DOES IT MEAN TO RELEASE THE PRESENCE OF GOD?

Releasing God's presence refers to releasing the presence of the Holy Spirit in every situation you may find yourself in. To be able to do this, you must be aware of the presence of the Holy Spirit and know He resides in you. What you become aware of you can release. You cannot manifest the Holy Spirit if you are not aware and conscious of Him. The ministry of the gospel of Jesus Christ is not a ministry of mere words but of releasing His presence on the earth. This ministry is important because God wants us to release His presence on all the earth. As Jesus walked around the earth, He was conscious of the power of God (the anointing) in Him, upon Him, and the presence of God in His life. That is why, when the woman with the issue of blood touched the hem of Jesus' garment, He was aware someone touched Him. He was very aware of the presence of the Holy Spirit.

God wants you to be aware of the Holy Spirit in and upon you. The more aware you are, the more practical it becomes for you to release Him, but you have to know Him as a person and talk to Him. To be able to release the divine presence of the Holy Spirit, you must be aware you are a carrier of God's divine presence. When you are ignorant of what you possess, you fail to write a check equal to what you have in the bank. So it is important to know what you have. You have the Holy Ghost inside you. You must be aware of His presence in your life because it is what you are aware of that you release into the atmosphere. Once you are aware the Holy Spirit lives in you, you can release Him everywhere you go.

> Heal the sick, raise the dead, cleanse the lepers, cast out demons. Freely you have received, freely give. (Matthew 10:8, AMP)

If you ask me what God has placed you here on the earth to do, my response would be to heal the sick, raise the dead, cleanse the lepers, and cast out demons. Yes, heal the sick, raise the dead, cleanse the lepers, and cast out demons. God says, freely you have received freely you give.

> Do not take gold, or silver, or [even] copper money in your money belt, or a provision bag for your journey, or even two tunics, or sandals, or a staff; for the worker deserves his support. Whatever city or village you enter, ask who in it is worthy [who welcomes you and your message], and stay at his house until you leave [that city]. As you go into the house, give it your greeting [that is, 'Peace be to this house']. If [the family living in] the house is worthy [welcoming you and your message], give it your [blessing of] peace [that is, a blessing of well-being and prosperity, the favor of God]. But if it is not worthy, take back your blessing of peace. (Matthew 10:9–13, AMP)

From this scripture, you see you can give what is in you. Jesus Christ told His disciples they could give peace and release the presence.

When you are aware of His presence, you can release it everywhere you go. The continuous release of God's presence on the earth results in the continuous experience of supernatural victory. If you want to experience victory in your life, release God's presence. If you want to experience victory at your place of work, release His presence into the atmosphere. Release His presence in your family, home, business, and life. The Bible tells us in the presence of God, mountains melt. In God's presence, no disease can stand. In God's presence, no difficulty can stand.

> The mountains melt like wax at the presence of the Lord, At the presence of the Lord of the whole earth. (Psalm 97:5, NKJV)

> The mountains quake at him, and the hills melt, and the earth is burned at his presence, yea, the world, and all that dwell therein. (Nahum 1:5)

The glory of the Lord is about to change your situation and circumstances. God's presence is in you, and as I release this word into your spirit and atmosphere, His presence is right where you are. It is important you understand you have been designated as a carrier of God's presence and you are meant to release it everywhere you go to change your atmosphere and world.

CHAPTER SEVEN

HOW TO RELEASE THE PRESENCE OF GOD

—

You may be asking yourself, "How can I release the presence of God?" I want to explain to you how certain things happen in the supernatural so you can operate the same way I do. God Has blessed me with an apostolic ministry where leaders are raised and taught how things work in the supernatural, so they may know it is not by coincidence, and they can also flow in the realm of the supernatural.

> In the last day, that great day of the feast, Jesus stood and cried, saying, If any man thirst, let him come unto me, and drink. He that believeth on me, as the scripture hath said, out of his belly shall flow rivers of living water. (John 7:37–38)

The scripture says, "If any man thirsts let him come unto me and drink." Are you thirsty? Do you want to know how to flow in the realm of the supernatural and release the presence of God everywhere you go?

The scripture also says, "He that believeth on me, as the scripture hath said, out of his belly shall flow rivers of living water." Notice the Bible says, out of your belly shall flow rivers, not a river. It is an unlimited spirit in the world of limited possibilities. Do you know the Spirit of God can give you speed for things to begin to happen much faster in your life than they are happening? When you engage the Spirit, you experience the speed. The more you release, the more you have speed.

Do you know you can do the works Jesus did and even greater (John 14:12)? The Bible tells us Jesus Christ is the Son of God (John 1:34). He is our elder brother (Romans 8:29). He is the Lion of the tribe of Judah (Revelation 5:5) and you are just like Him.

Sometimes you might wonder how Jesus did the things He did. How did He open blind eyes? How did He walk through His enemies but they could not even touch Him? How did He survive in the world where He was hated by so many? How did Jesus know who He was that He spoke boldly about it all the time? He said He is the Light (John 8:12). He said He is the Bread of Life (John 6:35). He said He is life (John 11:25). Jesus knew something the religious leaders of His time did not know. They wondered how He did the things He did. For instance, how He was able to get money out of the mouth of the fish (Matthew 17:27), turn water into wine (John 2:1–11), raise Lazarus from the dead (John 11:38–44), heal the sick (Matthew 4:23–25), and cast out devils (Luke 11:14). The secret is being in the presence of God. God wants us to have that kind of consciousness. Everywhere Jesus went He released the presence of God; He lived in the presence. This same Jesus wants you to operate just as He did.

Releasing God's presence comes in different degrees and stages There is a stage in your life God's presence can be released by words, which is important, and we learn how to do that in this book.

You release God's presence with your words by speaking into the atmosphere while being consciously aware of the presence of the Holy Spirit in you, and the divinity you carry in your humanity. You can release His presence with your words, but you must be aware and conscious of His presence when you are doing that.

As you progress in your relationship with God and spending time in His presence, the presence rubs off on you. Your presence alone exudes God's presence that is upon you without you even saying a word. Yes, you can also release God's presence by your mere presence while remaining conscious it is in or upon you. It is the consciousness and awareness of His presence in your life that brings about its continuous manifestation in your atmosphere. We see this in the story of Peter where the Bible says,

> Then Peter said, Silver and gold have I none; but such as I have give I thee: In the name of Jesus Christ of Nazareth rise up and walk. (Acts 3:6)

Because Peter knew what he possessed and was aware of God's presence in him, he was able to release it. As a result, the lame man began to walk. You must release what is inside you. The Holy Ghost (God's presence) resides in you, and you must be aware of this. Once you are aware of this, you can begin to release God's presence in the atmosphere. In God's presence there is healing and liberty; that is why when Peter released His presence, the lame man began to walk.

Let's look at another biblical demonstration of the release of God's presence:

> Insomuch that they brought forth the sick into the streets, and laid them on beds and couches, that at the least the shadow of Peter passing by might overshadow some of them. (Acts 5:15)

Right here, we can see the sick were healed by being overshadowed by Peter's shadow. That does not mean there was power in Peter's shadow. It means Peter was releasing the presence of God. It is important to note Peter did not say a word, but the sick were healed by his presence alone.

You reach a level in your walk in the supernatural where the presence of God is released by your presence alone (as in Peter's shadow), not because you are saying something. The presence you are under over-shadows you. If you are always aware of God's presence, you are always in His presence, so there is an overshadowing of that presence upon your life in that you just carry it everywhere you go. In this instance, the presence is released because you have been in the presence of God. In Psalm 91:1 the Bible says, "He that dwells in the secret place of the most high shall abide under the shadow of the Almighty." If you spend time in His secret place, you abide under His shadow, and you release the presence of who overshadows you.

Your presence releases the presence of who you represent. You can release the presence of the Holy Spirit because His presence overshadows you. There was a lady who had heart problems, back problems, and an infection in her thumb. Since I am always consciously aware of what I am carrying, when I appeared in the environment she was in, the presence of God was released and the infection in that lady's thumb dried up. The chest pain disappeared instantly, even without me praying for her. You carry the presence of who you represent and your shadow will release the presence of who overshadows you. So, it is very important for you to be aware of what you carry. Always be aware of God's presence that is in you.

> He that dwelleth in the secret place of the Most High shall abide under the shadow of the Almighty. (Psalm 91:1)

Take note of the statement, "shall abide under the shadow of the Almighty." Your shadow will release the presence of who overshadows you. If you are overshadowed by the presence of God; as you walk around, you release the presence of the one who overshadows you.

You are meant to release what and who rubs off on you. God's presence is upon you, it is also in you, and you are to release it. The presence of God is powerful, so releasing it gives you victory over the forces of the Enemy. To help you understand this better let me put it this way: releasing the presence of God can be compared to releasing the smell of cologne sprayed on your shirt everywhere you go. The more you are aware of the cologne you are wearing, the more you smell it because you are conscious of what you put on. The same applies to releasing the presence of God. The more you are conscious of the presence of the Holy Spirit in you, the more you release that presence everywhere you go. So, it is important to be aware of the presence of the Holy Spirit in you.

Releasing the presence of God brings about the miraculous in the realm of the supernatural. In Matthew 10:5–6, we see Jesus Christ ordained the twelve disciples and sent them out with a command saying,

> Do not go into the way of the Gentiles, and do not enter a city of the Samaritans. But go rather to the lost sheep of the house of Israel. (Matthew 10:5b–6, NKJV)

Jesus sent the disciples out to do the supernatural and told them to preach that the kingdom of God is at hand:

> And as you go, preach, saying, 'The kingdom of heaven is at hand.' Heal the sick, cleanse the lepers, raise the dead, cast out demons. Freely you have received, freely give. (Matthew 10:7–8, NKJV)

Please note, in this passage, Jesus did not tell the disciples to pray for the sick. He commanded them to heal the sick, which was possible by releasing the presence of who overshadowed them.

Your desire should be to get to the place where anyone who comes into your presence is impacted by the presence of God you carry. In Matthew 10:7–8, Jesus also commanded the disciples to cleanse the lepers, raise the dead, and cast out demons.

Say, "I cleanse the lepers, I raise the dead, I cast out demons."

The presence of God can also be released by releasing your spirit. To know how to do this, you must understand your human spirit and the Holy Spirit. Every person has a human spirit that is a distinct part of him/her. Your spirit is not the same as your body or soul. 1 Corinthians 6:17 tells us a person who is joined to the Lord is one spirit with Him. You have to understand this if you want to walk in the supernatural presence of God. When you are born again, the Holy Spirit comes to live in you. The two of you become one Spirit. 1 Corinthians 6:19 says your body becomes the temple of the Holy Ghost. This means God comes in and stays in it. He tabernacles in you.

The Holy Spirit is a person and can be quenched or grieved. You can annoy Him. Have you ever been annoyed by someone? Do you walk away or stay? The Holy Ghost cannot walk away. He has come to stay. Although He is grieved or quenched, He stays, though not excited. When you quench Him, you put Him in a position where He cannot move freely in you because you annoy Him with the things you say.

Ephesians 4:30 tells us not to grieve the Holy Spirit of God by whom we were sealed for the day of redemption. So don't grieve the Holy Spirit. If you do, you miss out on Him expressing Himself through you. When you praise the Holy Spirit and speak good words about Him, He gets excited. He lives in you, and you are joined with Him in communion, a form of relationship.

Say, "I am joined with the Holy Spirit in communion."

What does communion mean? To answer this question, let's look at 2 Corinthians 13:14,

> The grace of the Lord Jesus Christ, and the love of God,
> and the communion of the Holy Ghost, be with you all.
> Amen. (2 Corinthians 13:14)

"The grace of our Lord Jesus Christ" means our Lord is an administrator of grace. It also says, "And the communion of the Holy Ghost." This means the Holy Ghost is the administrator of fellowship. The word "communion" in this scripture refers to presence and fellowship. It refers to sharing together, active participation, and partnership. So, when you commune with the Holy Spirit, you have partnership with Him. He is my senior partner. I never walk by myself. Everything I do, He is part of it and actively participates in it. We are always talking to each other. I participate in releasing the Holy Spirit to impact others.

Say, "I am in partnership with the Holy Spirit."

Do you know what that means? This means the Holy Ghost is your senior partner; you walk together. What He brings to the table belongs to both of you. When you are part of a business, whatever your business partner brings in is for everybody who is part of the business.

Let's look at the same scripture in the Amplified Classic for a better rendering:

> The grace (favor and spiritual blessing) of the Lord Jesus Christ and the love of God and the presence and fellowship (the communion and sharing together, and participation) in the Holy Spirit be with you all. Amen (so be it). (2 Corinthians 13:14, AMPC)

Once you become a believer, the Holy Spirit comes to join you and there is partnership, sharing together, active participation, and fellowship with Him. As you surrender your thoughts, mind, and emotions to Him, you become one with Him, then the flow of the supernatural presence of God becomes normal in your life. The Holy Spirit flows through you as you yield to His prompting. If you are fighting with your partner, the relationship does not flow smoothly. When you yield to your senior partner (the Holy Spirit) there is a flow, so releasing the Holy Spirit becomes really easy.

You have a human Spirit, so you are a spirit-being. When you become a believer, your spirit and the Holy Spirit become one. So, when you release your spirit, you are releasing the Holy Spirit to flow through you. How do you release your spirit?

The Holy Spirit is sovereign. In 1 Corinthians 14:32, the Bible says, "The spirits of the prophets are subject to the prophets." You can decide to release what you have or keep it to yourself. When you release your spirit, the Holy Spirit flows through you and impacts whoever you are releasing Him upon. Hence, it is very important to be careful who you associate with because people can release on you whatever is operating in their spirits. For example, we know the spirit of anger is not of God, so being around someone who is full of anger will release the spirit of anger on you.

You may have been happy before you met the person but the moment you come into contact with him your attitude changes. This is because he has a bad spirit that is released from him to you. You release what is in you; you can only release from your spirit, not your mind or head.

Spiritual senses are different from the natural senses. Spiritual senses originate from your spirit and heart, not your head or mind. You must pay attention to that. In Proverbs 4:23, the Bible says, "Keep your heart with all diligence; for out of it are the issues of life."

The Spirit of God is in you. You and Jesus are one. In John 10:30, Jesus said He and the Father are one. In John 17:21, He said you are one with Him. Do you see that? In John 20:21, Jesus said as the Father has sent me, so have I sent you to release the presence of God.

To release the presence of God through your spirit, you must focus on what you are releasing; you cannot be distracted by everybody around you. If you want to release the presence of the Holy Spirit who dwells in you, you must yield to Him. This requires yielding to His desire, will, and person. When you get into a place, you should release God's presence into the atmosphere so whatever is not right in that place is brought under control by the released presence of God. You don't want to walk into a place and be overcome by the prevalent presence there.

God's Spirit being released through you is dependent on you, not God. It is when you yield yourself to Him, His will, and His desire that He flows out through you when you release your spirit. When the Spirit begins to flow, you will know something is coming out of you. If you want to heal the sick, you must be conscious of what you are releasing. When you are willing to give freely, the anointing is released through the Holy Spirit. When you hold back, the Holy Spirit is withheld because He is in you.

When it comes to releasing the presence of God, your heart is the key. You must know how your heart connects with your spirit in order to release the presence of God. Your heart comprises of your soul and spirit. In Proverbs 4:23, the Bible tells us, "Keep your heart with all diligence." To keep means, "to guard, to maintain, to protect, to watch over." Watch over your heart with all diligence because out of it are the issues of life. The heart is the core of a person, and the Bible says out of it are the issues of life. The flow comes out of your heart/spirit. So your heart's condition determines the flow of the presence of God from within. Of course, your mind has to also agree with your spirit.

To release the presence of God, your heart has to be in the right place. Therefore, you must stay focused on the presence of the one you want to release. When you do, the atmosphere changes and suddenly, something happens in you. Your spirit-man begins to release who you are focused on.

To release the presence of God, you must understand the work of your spirit and that of the Holy Spirit. Your spirit and the Holy Spirit are one, and the presence of God is in the realm of the spirit. Anything to do with God is in that realm also. When you understand how the spirit realm operates, you will always be in a place of authority and victory.

Spending time with the Holy Spirit develops your relationship and intimacy with Him; this makes it easier for you to release Him. I believe every believer has been endowed with the gift of the Spirit, so the Holy Spirit lives in every one of us. God wants you to release Him everywhere you go, but you must focus and direct your heart. Wherever you direct your heart, your spirit follows because they are connected. So to release healing, you must focus your heart with an agenda to release the presence of God that brings about healing. It has to be done intentionally. When you accept personal responsibility to heal the sick, your spirit flows and follows your heart. For instance, if I accept responsibility that I am the one to be used to bring healing to you, my spirit flows because I have accepted it as my responsibility.

Anywhere you find yourself is your place of influence, the area where God has positioned you to be; it is your location. Since you are in your location, you operate from there but you have to believe, focus your heart, and take personal responsibility. In Joshua 1:3, God told Joshua wherever the sole of his foot shall tread upon belongs to him.

> He that believeth on me, as the scripture hath said, out of his belly shall flow rivers of living water. (John 7:38)

As said before, the Holy Spirit is a person who lives inside you. He is one with your human spirit. Therefore, your human spirit has to be released to enable the Holy Spirit to be released. The Bible says, "out of his belly." That means, out of your spirit, which is joined to the Holy Spirt shall flow rivers of living water.

For more clarification, let's look at the same scripture from the NLT rendering,

> Anyone who believes in me may come and drink! For the Scriptures declare, 'Rivers of living water will flow from his heart.'" (When he said "living water," he was speaking of the Spirit, who would be given to everyone believing in him. But the Spirit had not yet been given, because Jesus had not yet entered into his glory.) (John 7:38–39, NLT)

Your spirit has spirit capacity; it is not limited like your body. In John 6:63, Jesus said, "The words that I speak are spirit." They are *pneuma*. Pneuma is a Greek word that means, "breath." Jesus knew what He was talking about. Every time Jesus stepped out to make things happen, there was an operation of the Holy Ghost.

God has given everyone a sphere of influence. When you release your flow, it changes the atmosphere of the territory God has given to you. A pastor's spirit flows over the church he pastors. Hence, if you find a church where the pastor is timid or speaks negatively, everybody in that place will be timid and negative. If you go to a church where there are no miracles, nobody in that church walks in miracles. If you go to a church where the pastor doesn't believe in tongues, nobody in that church speaks in tongues. This is because the pastor's spirit flows over the domain he has been given.

The same thing occurs with parents; their spirits flow over their children. That is why you see some children acting just like their parents, even though they are very young. The spirit of the parents is flowing over the children, making an impact on their actions, not because they were told what to do, but there is a flow. You have to be very careful of the environments you step into because the flow of the leader will overshadow you.

A believer's spirit can flow and impart life to others. Similarly, angry, hateful or prejudiced people also impart the spirits they carry to others. A leader who is always full of anger and vexation in the spirit imparts that spirit to those under his tutelage. The word "impart" means, "to release the same spirit on others." The Bible says, "He that believes, out of his belly shall flow." This means faith is to be exercised for supernatural activity to take place. To release the presence of God, you must believe when your spirit flows from within, the Holy Spirit is released. If you don't believe, there is no flow. Remember, there are three realms of the supernatural: faith, anointing, and presence. Faith is the legal entrance into the realm of the supernatural. It is a choice. You have to believe.

Say, "I believe there is a Holy Spirit. I believe the breath I breathe is the breath of the Holy Spirit."

Some people may say it is not so, but you believe and what you believe is what manifests.

> And these signs shall follow them that believe; In my name shall they cast out devils; they shall speak with new tongues. (Mark 16:17)

This scripture says, "And these signs shall follow them that believe," not just Christians. It is when you "believe" that you are able to move in the supernatural. You must believe; that's all it takes. There can be no supernatural without faith. Once again, the Spirit flows, but you must believe.

In Matthew 10:8, the disciples received the ministry of the supernatural freely, and Jesus told them to give it out freely. So, whatever you have received, it is your responsibility to give freely. You receive to give away. Every believer has the responsibility of giving away what God has put on the inside of them. As we deal with the presence of God, it is important to understand you must release it because the more you release the presence of God, the more the supernatural operates in your life.

> A spiritual gift is given to each of us so we can help each other. (1 Corinthians 12:7, NLT)

The King James Version of the same scripture puts it this way,

> But the manifestation of the Spirit is given to every man
> to profit withal. (1 Corinthians 12:7)

Spiritual gifts are given to each one of us so we can help each other. They are given to every man to profit withal. Every man includes you. It's every believer's privilege to be a channel of releasing the presence of God. God expects us to walk in the supernatural and if we are not, that means we are disobedient to God's command as His followers. He wants us to get people saved, heal the sick, cast out devils, and cleanse the lepers. This can only happen through the release of the presence of God.

Imagine if every Christian was aware of this and begins to release God's presence all over, imagine how our world would look today. Why don't you begin releasing God's presence in your life and everywhere you go? If you do, you will begin to experience supernatural victory. I challenge you today to remain aware of His presence that is in you. You carry the Holy Spirit in you; He is the breath of God, the Spirit of God, the ruach of God. Release Him by speaking and being consciously aware He resides in you. God wants you to release His presence every time, everywhere. Believe His power in your life and continually dwell in His presence.

CHAPTER EIGHT

THE MECHANISM OF RELEASING GOD'S PRESENCE

———

It is important to note the presence of God, and the supernatural, can be summoned at will and tangibly felt. Some Christians do not know this, but those who are serving the Devil know how to summon him.

If you know how the supernatural feels, you can always summon it at any time. People in the demonic realm summon demonic spirits to show up. Yet, Christians do not know as children of God they have the ability to summon the supernatural at will. I can say something will happen in a moment and it does because I summon the supernatural at will. You don't beg God saying, "Please, God, don't let us leave here today without experiencing your presence." No! We know all things work together for good to them that love God and are called according to His purpose (Romans 8:28). Expecting God to move is no coincidence. It is important you know this because it will help you in every area of your life: your relationships, finances, health, job interviews, and so forth. It will help to get a yes where it would have been a no.

Mechanical principles govern the supernatural and God's presence. These principles are relationship driven but the power aspect or the supernatural is fairly mechanical. This is similar to marriage counseling where the counselor gives a couple things to do, but they are based on a relationship. So they take the principles and submit them to an art form. It is all about your heart being established in Him.

There are three foundational truths involved in the mechanics or process of releasing the presence of God. These are:

1. Faith
   In Romans 10:17, the Bible says, "Faith comes by hearing and hearing by the Word of God." Faith comes by hearing the spoken living Word of God, the *rhema* Word quickened and delivered by God, not the letter of the Word of God in the Bible. Faith comes when you hear the energy-filled, living Word of God that has the power to awaken your heart.

   To release the presence of God you must have faith. You must also understand that faith can only provide what grace has made available. That means the presence of God has already been made available to you by grace but faith has to get hold of it. Jesus has already paid the price for you as a Christian, so you can delve into the realm of the supernatural and begin to operate in a dimension only those who understand that realm can operate in. It is by the grace of God so you cannot boast. Once you know what God has made available for and to you, you go for it and believe you can do it.

2. Awareness
   This is the foundation for releasing God's presence. You must become conscious of God's presence both mentally and sensually; this is not just in your mind but also in your senses. That means you need

to get sensitized to His presence. This will take developing new sets of senses. It starts with sensing a premonition, a very subtle feeling or a "gut" feeling.

So how do you sense the presence of God in your life?

Sensing the presence of God could start as a gut feeling. You may feel something rumble in your belly. This gut feeling is different from your five senses. It starts with a premonition. You should begin to listen loud and amplify what you are hearing. You then learn to become sensitive to the supernatural workings, which over time, become very detectable in that you learn to become sensitive when the presence is about to be released. You learn to become sensitive when God is about to do something through you. Over time, you can easily detect when the supernatural is about to take place. As we honor the presence of God and are thankful for little things, we invite more of His presence.

As you become faithful in releasing little, more is given. As you receive more of the presence of God, you can release more and more and more of that presence from your spirit. At first, it is dim and quiet. Then, by reason of use, you develop sensitivity, and it gets loud and clear.

> But strong meat belongeth to them that are of full age, even those who by reason of use have their senses exercised to discern both good and evil. (Hebrews 5:14)

It is by reason of use your senses are exercised to discern the difference between good and evil. The more you use what you have, the more you become better at it. The more you proactively wait upon the Lord, the more you sharpen your senses. The more you sharpen your senses, the more you begin to hear the Holy Spirit and have experiences you have never had before. Things begin to happen in your life; changes take place, and you learn how to change your world.

This is not only for pastors; it is for everyone. There was a man in the Bible whose name was Stephen. Stephen was not an apostle, but the Bible says he was filled with the Holy Ghost (Acts 6:5).

3. Distribution

   Distribution is the flow. It is important you understand you can release the flow. When you sense or feel the flow of the presence of God on the inside, you can move it by releasing Him from within. You cannot release what you don't have on the inside. That means, the presence of God can be moved or pushed out from within you by faith. There is a push, and something comes out that affects the person you are releasing to. It has to be done by faith, having consciousness of the Holy Spirit's presence in your life. You are filled with the Spirit of God, which means, you can push from within. You and God are one. You are like two liquids mixed together; therefore, you are inseparable. It is like water and dye; you are a moving, living house of God.

   You can release that presence of God over your finances, relationships, children, life, health, and over anything you want to. Can you imagine what will happen with your life if you apply what you know now? This information is not only for you to use on others, but it is also for you to apply it to your own life.

   Years ago, I used to wait for God to move before I moved. Sometimes, I would wait for a while. Then one day, the Lord gave me a revelation. He told me, "When you move, I move." That single revelation changed my ministry all together. Now, I just know when I move God moves because I am His extension. I am His hand, His feet, His eyes, His mouthpiece. He talks through me, so I just move and do what I have to do because I believe it. When I move, He moves and when I talk, He is talking.

   Say, "When I move God moves."

Many of you are waiting for God; yet, God is waiting on you. When you go out and start praying for the sick, you are moving; so God will move, and people will get healed. You cast out devils from those who are demon-possessed. You don't say, "God, should I cast the Devil out?" No! When you move, God moves. God wants you to be in charge of your life.

CHAPTER NINE

KEYS TO RELEASING THE PRESENCE OF GOD

––––––

1. Accept Responsibility

    You've got to accept responsibility. Accepting responsi-
    bility is saying, "In order for you to be free, it has to take
    me to set you free." In my home, I take responsibility;
    nothing is expected to go out of control. I just know I
    am responsible for what goes on there.

    Say, "I am responsible for what happens in my loca tion."

    In Deuteronomy 11:24a, God told Joshua whatever his
    feet stepped on, he would possess. That means wherever
    you go, you have influence over the spirits in that place.

Every place where you set your foot will be yours:
(Deuteronomy 11:24a, NIV)

You must accept responsibility for your measure or limited position.

> We, however, will not boast beyond measure, but within
> the limits of the sphere which God appointed us—a
> sphere which especially includes you. For we are not
> overextending ourselves (as though our authority did
> not extend to you), for it was to you that we came with
> the gospel of Christ. (2 Corinthians 10:13–14, NKJV)

2 Corinthians 10:14 tells us we do not stretch beyond our measure/
sphere of authority/influence God has given us. A father's sphere of
influence is his family. He has authority over his children whenever
he embraces and exercises it. You can tell your child you are blessed
from now on, and that child will walk in such a blessing when you
say it from your heart. In 2 Corinthians 10:13, apostle Paul wrote to
the Corinthian church telling them not to boast beyond their measure, but within the limits of the sphere which God appointed them.

Say, "I have a limit."

The most important thing for you to do as God's child is to discover
your sphere of influence and authority and release the presence of
God on those within that sphere. God gives you a sphere where you
can exert authority releasing the presence. Your measure is like a
limited position or a sphere of activity, which God has given you
responsibility for. Each person has a unique measure or a sphere of
respect and responsibility.

Parents influence their children and business people influence their
businesses. You can talk to your business. If I talk to your business,
it is because you have given me the authority, and when I speak to
it, it will begin to prosper because you have told me to take over and

speak. If you, as the owner of the business, do not invite me to declare and release into the business, I have no authority in that sphere.

Do you know when your children go to school, you have no control over them while they are in the custody of their teacher? They are under the sphere of the influence of their teachers, and they must respond to the authority exerted by their teacher.

You should take initiatives within the location of your influence and step out to bring change. You cannot allow things to go the way they are going without bringing change, especially if they are under your authority. Once you have discovered what God has given you responsibility for, you must first of all take the responsibility, then embrace it, and release the presence of God into what He has entrusted to you.

Say, "I believe if things must change in my household, it depends on me."

That is a major responsibility. Essentially, you are saying, if my family becomes very blessed, it will depend on me. When you say that, something changes completely. This is because you have taken responsibility for your space and have become responsible. Don't wait for someone to do it; step up and begin to do what nobody has done. The things God has entrusted to you as your location (sphere of influence) to exercise the supernatural are your life (you are the best prophet of your destiny), home, finances, relationships, and work. God has given you authority over all these.

Say, "My life is in my hands."

This may not sound religious, but it is true. It is easier to say, "My life is in Your hands." That would be religion. You are a very important person when it comes to your destiny. The decisions you make determine how far you go in life, so you have a big role to play.

So, who is influencing you?

If you fail to apply or release God's divine supernatural ability of His presence on your life, relationships, family, finances, home, and business, something will exercise spiritual authority over them. You've got to rise up, learn these keys, and accept responsibility for what God has given to you, so you can change your life.

2. Embrace Your Sphere of Influence with Love and Faith
    When you say, "If things are going to change in my family and/or in my business, it depends on me," you are embracing your sphere of influence with love and faith. When you do that, your spirit-man awakens and something changes completely because you have taken responsibility for your space. You have to accept your sphere of influence and love the way God has positioned you. The presence of God flows better in the atmosphere of love and faith because love releases the presence of God through faith. When God's presence flows out of love, there is purity in the flow, and it brings healing and deliverance because there is love in motion. Let's look at Philippians 1:6–7:

    > Being confident of this very thing, that he which hath begun a good work in you will perform it until the day of Jesus Christ: Even as it is meet for me to think this of you all, because I have you in my heart; inasmuch as both in my bonds, and in the defense and confirmation of the gospel, ye all are partakers of my grace. (Philippians 1:6–7)

    Philippians 1:7 says, "I have you in my heart." Wherever your heart is directed, your spirit flows. Apostle Paul was absolutely confident, and he exhibited total inner passion. He was confident of the Spirit of God working among the believers because he had them in his heart. Apostle Paul held those believers in his heart and released the apostolic anointing on them. Never give up or let go any of your children from your heart, regardless of the circumstances surrounding them. The grace of God flows in the direction of whom you hold in your heart in love. To see the flow of the supernatural presence of God from your heart to your sphere of influence, you must hold it in your heart with love and faith.

3. Speak Words
    Jesus tells us:

> The words that I speak to you are spirit, and they are life. (John 6:63b)

Words spoken are spirit and life. Life is more spiritual than physical. You can change circumstances in your life by your words.

Say, "I can change my circumstances by the power of the Holy Spirit."

Because words are spirits, you can make up your mind to engage the spirit world and change that circumstance in your life by speaking words to it. Speak to that situation. Speak to your body. Speak to your finances (your bank account). Speak! Since words are spirits, what you speak impacts what happens in your life, but you must believe your words.

Say, "I believe what I say."

Believe and hold onto your words. Words spoken from within your heart release spiritual power because words are spirits. Words spoken from your head are empty. When you talk and about five seconds later you don't remember what you said, that is empty talk. That means your mind was not there. You were absent-minded because your heart was not in what you were saying.

Words are containers of power. So, when you release words, they release power. Words are seeds. You plant a word and within a matter of time, it germinates into a tree. You are where you are today because of what you have been saying about yourself and your life. That is why you are to change your vocabulary the moment you become a Christian.

Many Christians still talk the way they used to talk before they got born again. This is because they were not taught to change their vocabulary. The first thing you change when you are born again is your vocabulary because words are spirits. If you are in the right church, they start teaching you to change your vocabulary the moment you become a Christian because if you don't change your words, your life will not change. It all starts with your words. The Christian walk is not about dos and don'ts. You can follow all the dos and don'ts, but your words will still kill you unless you change your vocabulary.

Words spoken can release life or death. Don't be in a place where the words of death are being released all the time. If you are in a church where the pastor is always speaking words of death or says, "Things will never go right, and life is hard"—get out! The more you sit there, the more those words will be released into your spirit and you will get weaker and weaker because words release life or death.

> Death and life are in the power of the tongue: and they
> that love it shall eat the fruit thereof. (Proverbs 18:21)

This scripture says, "Death and life are in the power of the tongue." This means your life is dependent on what you say. You can release death or life. Words can release the Holy Spirit or demonic spirits, depending on what you say. Everything you say has a spirit behind it. Whatever is spoken from your mouth can release the spirit of God or the Devil. You can go to some churches and leave more scared than you were before you went there. This is because of the words released into your spirit. It is important you get this because being a Christian does not mean you cannot release demonic spirits. Remember, Peter was Jesus' disciple; yet, he spoke some things and Jesus said to him,

"Get thee behind me, Satan" (Matthew 16:22–23). That is why you have to fill yourself with the Word of God and watch what you say.

As a Christian, you must watch your heart with all diligence. Watch what you say; it can produce life or death. You release good presence or bad presence, the Holy Ghost or demonic spirits by the words you speak.

Words are meant to be spoken. Nothing moves until words are released because words are dynamite. In Mark 11:23, the Bible tells us to speak to the mountain to be removed and not doubt in our hearts. Do you have some mountains in your life? Talk to them; do not talk about the mountains. Do not display the mountains on your Facebook status.

> For verily I say unto you, That whosoever shall say unto this mountain, Be thou removed, and be thou cast into the sea; and shall not doubt in his heart, but shall believe that those things which he saith shall come to pass; he shall have whatsoever he saith. (Mark 11:23)

Words spoken in faith exert spiritual pressure on people, demons, and circumstances.

What does it mean to speak in faith?

Just believe what you say. Don't speak empty words. Going forward, believe what you say and say what you believe. Don't withdraw from your words; stand behind them with expectation. It doesn't matter how long it takes to see the manifestation; stand by those words and keep on saying them until you see the manifestation because words release power.

In Matthew 16:19, the Bible says words bind demonic spirits. If you have demonic spirits disturbing you, your words can bind and lock them.

> And I will give unto thee the keys of the kingdom of
> heaven: and whatsoever thou shalt bind on earth shall
> be bound in heaven: and whatsoever thou shalt loose on
> earth shall be loosed in heaven. (Matthew 16:19)

Demons are not humans; they are spirits, and spirits bind spirits.
Your words are spirits, so they can bind demonic spirits. You don't
war against flesh and blood; you don't tie demonic spirits with a rope
using your hands. It won't work. The words you speak put demonic
spirits in their place.

In the realm of the spirit, words are very important. Just as words
bind demon spirits, they also release God's presence. That is why
the Bible tells us in Revelation 12:11, we overcome by the blood of
the Lamb and the word of our testimony.

> And they overcame him by the blood of the Lamb, and
> by the word of their testimony; and they loved not their
> lives unto the death. (Revelation 12:11)

From this scripture, we see the blood and the word mix, and according to John 1:1, we know the Word is Jesus.

> In the beginning was the Word, and the Word was with
> God, and the Word was God. (John 1:1)

Jesus is the Word, so anytime you open your mouth to speak, you
are speaking Him, the Word, Jesus. He is powerful. However, you
must have the consciousness that your words carry weight.

> You carry the presence of God and you can release it
> with words. Let's look at Matthew 10:11–14:

And into whatsoever city or town ye shall enter, enquire who in it
is worthy; and there abide till ye go thence. And when ye come into
an house, salute it. And if the house be worthy, let your peace come

upon it: but if it be not worthy, let your peace return to you. And whosoever shall not receive you, nor hear your words, when ye depart out of that house or city, shake off the dust of your feet.

In this scripture, Jesus told the disciples, whatever city or town you enter, ask who is responsible and stay there. When you come into the house, "salute" the household. This means, "Speak and release peace into the household." They had to say something in order to release the presence. When Jews meet, they release peace by saying Shalom. Jesus told the disciples, "If the household is worthy, let your peace come upon it, but if it is not worthy, let your peace return to you, and when you depart, shake off the dust from your feet because they did not receive you."

Basically, Jesus was telling the disciples if they receive you well, you release the presence, and if they don't receive you, take it back and get out of there. That means you carry something you can give to somebody or take it back if you are not received or accepted. Yes, you are a custodian of God's presence, and you have the ability to give it or take it back.

Having the awareness and the knowledge you are a custodian and a carrier of God's presence, and you can give or take it back, puts you at an advantage. If you find people who carry His presence, connect with them because what they carry has the ability to rub off on you. This is why the Bible tells us in Proverbs 22:24–25, do not associate yourself with an angry man; otherwise, you will become as angry as he is.

Jesus said you can give out what you have. You can release the peace and presence with your words. It is not a magic formula you create and hope God shows up. No, you know who is in you. There is no maybe. Remember God's presence can be summoned because it is already in you. One may ask, so what kind of spoken words release the presence of God?

> Let no corrupt word proceed out of your mouth, but
> what is good for necessary edification, that it may im-
> part grace to the hearers. (Ephesians 4:29, NKJV)

If you speak corrupt words, you cannot release the divine presence
of God on people because out of the same spring cannot come forth
both fresh and salt water (James 3:11). You cannot be bitter all day
long and expect to release God's presence effectively and efficiently.
This scripture tells us when you speak words that build up people,
encourage them, and make them solidified, these kinds of words
impart grace. Grace is the supernatural power and presence of God.
So when you speak words of honor, they impart, release, and deposit
grace into people's lives. If you do this all the time, you carry lots of
His presence in your life.

God is good all the time. God is light; there is no darkness in Him.
You cannot be speaking words of darkness all the time and expect
to release the presence of God; it cannot happen! God is peace. God
is love. God is joy. So that means every word you speak has to line
up with the character of God to bring about the release of God's
presence everywhere you go. You can no longer just say, "That is just
the way I am." No, you have to be an imitator of Jesus.

You should become godlier, talking like Jesus, thinking like Jesus,
and having Christ consciousness. That means from now on, speak
words of grace that will impact other people's lives regardless of what
they have done. No matter what you do, release grace on people, be
full of grace in your words. When you do that, you become an em-
bodiment of God's presence and everywhere you go, the presence is
released because there is so much grace. But if you are always speaking corrupt words, those words don't impart grace on people; they
don't release God's presence. Instead, they energize demonic spirits.
You don't want to be an energizer of demonic spirits; you want your
words to activate the Holy Ghost.

Words of truth (God's Word) that are spoken boldly release His presence. When you speak words of truth, the anointing of the Holy Spirit is released. Every time you speak the word of truth, you release the presence of God. The intensity might not be that high but you are releasing presence at the level you are walking at. We are all at different levels. So what I am teaching you is to bring you to the level where I am. As you are going higher, I am going higher as well. God wants all of us to increase in His presence and the anointing. It has to be done with authority. You must believe you've got it, and speak the word of truth boldly.

Peter and John knew they carried the presence of God. In Acts 3:4–9, Peter and John were going to the temple when a certain man, born lame, and who lay daily at the gate of the temple, asking alms of them. Peter said, "Look on us." Peter was trying to get the man's attention to focus on him because you receive from what you focus on.

Don't ever feel as if you are a nobody; you have something inside of you. Just tell someone to focus on you; then, release the presence of God. If you can get them to focus on you, you can then release to what you focus on. When you are to be prayed for or receive impartation of the supernatural, just receive what is being released. It is not time to ask for what you need, unless you have been asked to do so. Just receive. Focus and say, "God, I have come to receive, and whatever is about to be released, I want to take it in." Your focus should be on what you are about to receive.

4. Seize Every Opportunity to Pray
   Anytime you get an opportunity to pray for others, seize it because the more you pray for people, the more the presence grows and develops in you. When someone is sick, ask if you can pray for him or her. The more you do this for the reason of use, the more the release of the presence of God increases and strengthens.

But strong meat belongeth to them that are of full age,
even those who by reason of use have their senses exercised to discern both good and evil. (Hebrews 5:14)

The Holy Spirit lives in you. The two of you are one in fellowship,
in partnership, in relationship, and you can consciously release the
presence of God.

If you do what I have shared with you, you can heal the sick, raise
the dead, cast out devils, and cleanse the lepers because the power
is in you. Don't go through life without expressing divinity out of
your humanity. Don't go through life allowing what God has put in
you to go to waste. Don't allow the impartation you have received
go without releasing it. You must give expression to that power that
resides in you and release the presence. The more it is released, the
more you see the supernatural presence of God at work in your life.

God wants us to be constantly filled with the spirit, so we can release
His presence. The more it is released, the more we are filled. If you
keep it to yourself, it will become stagnant. I want you to pray that
God gives you the grace and opportunities to continue to release His
presence in your life.

I like what Peter says in Acts 3:6, "Such as I have I give unto you."
You've got something in you. You have the presence of God working
in you. But you must give expression to it!

CHAPTER TEN

HOSTING THE PRESENCE OF GOD

It is God's plan and purpose that we not only live in His presence and release it but also host His presence. When I talk about hosting the presence of God, I am referring to the presence of God being and remaining in us. We know a host is someone who welcomes somebody into his or her home. We have the distinct privilege and honor to host the presence of God! Just think about God trusting human beings like you and me so much He put His Spirit in us. Just let it soak into your spirit. In Ezekiel 36:27 God says,

> And <u>I will put my spirit within you</u>, and cause you to walk in my statutes, and ye shall keep my judgments, and do them. (Ezekiel 36:27)

God said He will put His Spirit in you so you can host Him. God wants us to host Him. Why? Because He trusts us and cares about us.

It is not because of anything we did, or how we acted, but because of His great love for us.

Hosting the presence of God means being a carrier of God's presence. It is quite sobering when I think of the fact that God would allow us to host His presence. Just take a moment and think about it. The thought of God allowing you and me to host His presence literally transforms my life. As God's children, we must understand the fact that we are carriers of God's presence. Remember there are three aspects of God's presence:

1. The omnipresence of God
2. The indwelling presence of God
3. The manifest presence of God

THE OMNIPRESENCE OF GOD

God is omnipresent. That means He is everywhere. There is no place you can go that God is not already there. This is why David said,

> Whither shall I go from thy spirit? or whither shall I flee
> from thy presence? If I ascend up into heaven, thou art
> there: if I make my bed in hell, behold, thou art there.
> (Psalm 139:7–8)

This scripture shows us God is with us; His presence is very near us.

THE INDWELLING PRESENCE OF GOD

The indwelling presence is the presence of the Holy Spirit you receive upon salvation and resides in you.

> In him you also, when you heard the word of truth, the
> gospel of your salvation, and believed in him, were sealed
> with the promised Holy Spirit, (Ephesians 1:13, ESV)

All those who are born again have the Holy Spirit living in them because they were sealed with Him unto the day of redemption. The presence of God lives in you; you are a carrier or host of God's indwelling presence.

> Do you not know that you are God's temple and that
> God's Spirit dwells in you? (1 Corinthians 3:16, ESV)

It is God's desire for you to not only host His indwelling presence but also host His manifest presence upon your life.

THE MANIFEST PRESENCE OF GOD

The manifest presence of God is the tangibility of God's glory evident upon and around us.

In the Old Testament, the Ark of the Covenant was the symbol for the manifest presence of God on the earth. The priests carried the Ark of the Covenant wherever they went. In the New Testament, the Bible tells us in Revelation 1:6 that Jesus has made us kings and priests of the Most High. In 1 Peter 2:9, the Bible tells us we are a chosen generation and a royal priesthood. So now we are priests unto God; hence, carriers of His presence. This privilege and assignment is something we must learn how to effectively guard and protect. God has decided to allow you to be a carrier of His manifest presence wherever you go. The indwelling presence is wonderful, but when you carry His manifest presence, it changes the atmosphere around you.

2 Timothy 1:14 tells us we should carefully guard the good deposit that has been entrusted to us by the help of the Holy Spirit. God wants us to understand how to host Him. He is letting us know as the hosts of His presence, we have to guard Him. The indwelling presence of the Spirit of God that resides in you is for your sake until it is released, but the manifest presence of God on you is for others. When you host His manifest presence, you will release that presence into your atmosphere resulting in a change in the atmosphere where you are present.

HOSTING HIS MANIFEST PRESENCE IN OUR LIVES

Manifesting God's presence in our lives is just as important as being a carrier of God's presence. Let's look at a few scriptures in the book of Psalms that demonstrate how to host the presence of God and how to make it manifest in our lives,

> My eyes are continually toward the LORD,
> For He will pluck my feet out of the net. (Psalm 25:15, NASB)

> But <u>my eyes are fixed on you, Sovereign LORD</u>;
> in you I take refuge—do not give me over to death. (Psalm 141:8, NIV)

> <u>I keep my eyes always on the LORD</u>.
> With him at my right hand, I will not be shaken. (Psalm 16:8, NIV)

In these scriptures, we see the common phrase is that David's eyes were fixed on the Lord. We know David was a man after God's own heart because he diligently searched for God's presence. He always wanted to have God's manifest presence on His life. This manifested in David's life in such a way that God's presence was always with him. So now, we are going to learn from David how to host the presence of the Lord, and how to manifest it in our lives.

In the above scriptures, we see three similar phrases that point to David's attentiveness to God: "My eyes are continually toward the LORD" (Psalm 25:15a, NASB). "My eyes are fixed on you, Sovereign LORD" (Psalm141:8a, NIV) and "I keep my eyes always on the LORD" (Psalm 16:8a, NIV). You will look at whatever you give your attention to and whatever you look at gets your attention. What you focus on becomes your focus; therefore, as a child of God, whatever you look at you receive from. Now, as you read the contents of this book, you are receiving something from me. When your eyes are continuously looking toward God, something begins to happen; you receive from Him. When you gaze upon an image, it is installed in you. Similarly, as you gaze on Jesus, the Holy Spirit, and God, you receive the very image of God installed in you, and the presence of God begins to manifest upon your life. We have to gaze upon the Lord.

When your attention is not on God, you cannot become like Him. You are transformed into the image you look at. To get the manifest presence of God upon your life, you must keep your attention and focus on God. As you look unto God and gaze your eyes on the Master, you become more like Him. In 2 Corinthians 3:18, the Bible tells us as we put our attention on the person we are hosting, we become like that person.

> But we all, with open face beholding as in a glass the glory of the Lord, are changed into the same image from glory to glory, even as by the Spirit of the Lord. (2 Corinthians 3:18)

The glory of the Lord rests upon us as we look upon Him. If we want to experience God's manifest presence and His glory resting on us, we must look at Him. When you gaze at the Word of God, the glory of the Word comes upon you and you manifest His presence in your life, transforming you into His very image. As you focus your eyes on God and look to Jesus, remember the person of God includes His presence and voice. As you look at the Word of God, you are turned into the same image you are beholding. His person is His Word and in His Word is His presence and His voice.

To continuously turn your eyes unto the Lord is to give your attention to His presence. As you look unto His Word, you are giving your attention to His presence. As you give your attention to His presence, you receive His manifest presence upon your life. When you give attention to His voice, you receive His voice. Whatever you give attention to is what manifests in your life. As you give attention to His person, you are hosting His presence, which is manifested in your life. We just read in the book of Psalms we have to continually look to the Lord. The word "continually" means, "Fix your gaze on Him all the time." When you continually gaze on God, you begin to host His presence on your life. You host whoever you gaze at. When your gaze is not on the Lord, you lose His attentiveness and awareness. Hence, you will not experience all the presence that can be imparted into your life as it would if you keep your eyes focused on God.

As you give your attention to God continually, you begin to host His presence upon you. As you look at Him and gaze at the person of Jesus, you will not only begin to experience His presence upon your life, but you will also hear His voice. Whatever you look at manifests in your life. God wants you to become attentive to His face. As you look at Him and gaze your eyes upon the Master, you become more like Him. You are transformed into His image. God wants you not to just host the indwelling presence, but also host the manifest presence wherever you go. This is because when you host His manifest presence, you carry it on you and you change the atmosphere around you.

You are a world changer who changes your environment. In order to change the atmosphere effectively, you must carry the manifest presence of God. You do this by fixing your eyes on Him. The best way to look at Him is to look into His Word. As you look into His Word, you become more like Him because whatever you give your attention, you attract. Whatever image you look at gets transposed into your own life.

God wants you to walk in His presence and do things out of His presence, not just out of His principle. The principle of Jesus will give you success, but the person of Jesus will change everything around you. The person of Jesus will change the circumstances in your life and the people around you. The person of Jesus will change your region, city, and nation. God's presence brings about transformation. God's presence brings about change. If you want a change in the lives of those around you, why don't you consciously host His presence upon your life?

So the secret of hosting God's presence is beholding Him and giving your attention to Him continually by paying attention to His Word and the person of Jesus Christ. As you pay attention to the person of Jesus Christ, you will have a remarkable experience greater than your wildest imaginations.

HOW TO CARRY YOURSELF AS A HOST OF GOD'S PRESENCE

As a host of God's presence, you ought to carry yourself with the awareness the Greater One lives in you and the Spirit of God is upon you. The presence of God should affect the things you say and also have an impact on who you choose to relate to on a personal level.

God wants you to host His presence, not just in you, but also upon you. I think of John 1:29, when John the Baptist saw Jesus coming to him and said, "Behold the lamb of God which taketh away the sin of the world." The Bible tells us John saw the Spirit descending from heaven like a dove, and it abode upon Jesus. Please note God's Spirit is not a dove but He descended upon Jesus "like a dove". In other words, He descended the way a dove would descend. The moment the Spirit of the Lord came from heaven, it was opened for you to experience the manifest presence of God on your life.

> Then John gave this testimony: I saw the Spirit come down from heaven as a dove and remain on him. (John 1:32, NIV)

The Spirit of God wants to remain on you. You are a host of His presence, not just in you but upon you. As you host Him in your life, wherever you go, the atmosphere changes because of the presence of God on you. If you enter a place that is full of chaos, the moment you step in, peace will show up.

I challenge you right now to fix your eyes on Jesus. Fix your eyes on the Word of God. Fix your eyes on God's Spirit that lives in you. Fix your eyes and mind on the King of kings and the God of heaven. As you gaze into His awesomeness, His power and His greatness, what you are gazing at begins to come upon you. When it comes upon you, you become a carrier and host of His presence, in you and upon you. As a carrier and host of the Spirit of the living God, you start changing your world and the things around you

God wants us to camp around His presence. The Bible tells us in the presence of God there is fullness of joy and pleasures forever more. It is very important that as we deal with this topic on God's presence, your hunger to be in His presence, to release His presence and to host His presence increases. There is a song that says, "Your presence is heaven to me." This should be the mindset of every child of God.

CHAPTER ELEVEN

CULTIVATING THE PRESENCE OF GOD

————

What does cultivating the presence of God mean or look like?

Cultivating God's presence means to develop His presence in your life and acquire the skill of consistently being aware of it upon your life. Learning how to cultivate God's presence in your life sets you apart from others. The difference between you and other people is not so much about what you or they know, but how much of God's presence is upon your life or their lives.

Cultivating the presence of God is not just limited to your prayer life. However, it is important to know the way you pray changes when you learn to cultivate His presence in your life. Most people often think they always have to set aside a time for prayer, which is very import-ant; however, when you cultivate His presence, your prayer lifestyle completely changes. You begin to pray without ceasing because you are constantly in communion with the Holy Spirit throughout the day. The art of cultivating God's presence should be a lifestyle for every believer.

It is God's plan and purpose for His presence to rest upon your life and you live your life from His presence. Living your life from His presence also means living your life from the inside of you, instead of the outside.

When you live life from the outside, you are like a thermometer which allows the environment to control its readings. When the temperature in the environment rises, the thermometer's temperature also rises, and when it cools down, the thermometer's temperature also goes down. You allow the circumstances of life to control you. When going through trials, you are filled with turmoil but when there are no trials, you are at peace.

When you live your life from the inside, you are like a thermostat, which controls the temperature of its environment. When the temperature rises, the thermostat turns on the air conditioner to cool down the environment. On the other hand, when the temperature drops, it turns on the heat to warm up the environment. A practical example would be whether you are going through trials or not, you have constant peace. You consistently and confidently remain the same regardless of what is going on around you because you trust God, have confidence in His power, and believe in His Word. In essence, living from the outside is living by your senses. However, living life from the inside is walking or living by faith.

When you start living your life from the inside, you begin to cultivate God's presence in your life. I pray that as you read this book, you begin to develop some skills of cultivating His presence. When you think about a problem over and over again that is referred to as worry. God does not want you to live your life like that; He does not want you to worry. When you think about the Word of God over and over again that is called meditation; you ponder and dwell on it in your heart. When you think about the Lord over and over again, you are cultivating His presence in your life.

One may ask, "How do I think about God?"

Think about His love; think about His provision; think about His protection; think about His person; think about the answers He has given to your prayers in the past. When you think about the Lord, it brings a change in your life. God's presence should mean everything to you. God's presence is more powerful than anything else in this world because in His presence, there is the evidence of peace; in His presence is pleasure; in His presence there is fullness of joy. His presence is what sets you apart from the people of the world. His presence is what differentiates you from somebody who is just a churchgoer. When you begin to cultivate His presence in your life, great things begin to happen.

> Blessed are those who have learned to acclaim you, who walk in the light of your presence, LORD. (Psalm 89:15, NIV)

Walking in the light of God's presence is cultivating God's presence. This brings you to a place of blessing in the presence of the Lord.

> One thing I ask from the LORD, this only do I seek: that I may dwell in the house of the LORD all the days of my life, to gaze on the beauty of the LORD and to seek him in his temple. (Psalm 27:4, NIV)

How radiant is God to you? How beautiful is the Lord to you? Gaze on His beauty. Seek God in His temple. When you focus your mind and thoughts on His presence, you begin to cultivate and experience it in a greater dimension all the days of your life. It is God's plan and purpose that His presence becomes more important to you than anything. You are not just carrying His presence in you, but there is also an emanation of His presence in you as a result of cultivating His presence in your life. God told Moses,

> My presence will go with you, and I will give you rest. (Exodus 33:14, NIV)

When God's presence goes with you, you have rest. When you cultivate God's presence by focusing your mind on it, it brings you rest. People with unrest in their lives are very likely missing the ingredient of God's presence. No one can carry God's presence and have a chaotic life. The moment unrest shows up in your spirit, it is an indication that the measure of God's presence you are carrying upon your life is not the measure God wants you to carry. You must cultivate God's presence in your life and develop it in your time of prayer and thought life. When you think about the Lord all the time, the radiance of His presence begins to manifest in your life because whoever you think about the most forms their image in your mind. As you look on God's Word, its image is transposed into your life.

> But whose delight is in the law of the LORD, and who meditates on his law day and night. (Psalm 1:2, NIV)

To cultivate God's presence, you must focus on Him day and night. Whenever you are awake, whatever you are doing, think on His presence.

> That person is like a tree planted by streams of water, which yields its fruit in season and whose leaf does not wither— whatever they do prospers. (Psalm 1:3, NIV)

Do you want to prosper in your life? Do you want to experience prosperity in your soul, mind, and the work of your hand? If the answer is yes, think on the Word of God. Cultivate the presence of the Holy Spirit in your life. As you cultivate His presence by meditating on His Word, you will experience rest and prosperity.

The key to cultivating His presence is not about changing what you do but changing your attitude toward what you do. Whatever you do, do it as unto the Lord; have the attitude God is always with you. Cultivate His presence in whatever you do, even in your place of work, business, relationships, eating, and conversations. Let God be your primary focus in all you do. When you begin to do that, you are in the journey of cultivating His presence in your life because everything you do is linked to His presence. It is no longer about you; it becomes all about Him. Your life takes a new form and dimension because His presence is being cultivated in it. We see this in Colossians 3:23,

Whatever you do, work at it with all your heart, as working for the Lord, not for human masters. (NIV)

As you cultivate God's presence, putting God first in every area of your life, you will experience a different dimension of His presence in your life.

The Bible says the Holy Spirit has been given to us without measure (John 3:34). That means His presence has been given to us without measure; however, we set the limit on it in our lives. So how do you raise that limit of the measure of God's presence upon your life?

Whatever you jealously guard is the measure you will have on a consistent basis. The Bible tells us when you are faithful with what you have been given, you experience more in your life (Matthew 25:23). All measurement in God's kingdom exists for us to pursue an increase. As you cultivate His presence, you pursue an increase of His presence in your life.

How would you feel if God's presence is so evident upon your life that wherever you go everybody sees it? Even your enemy will know you are carrying God's presence. Use what you have now; be aware of His presence and jealously guard it. Think about the Lord; stop thinking about your problem as that leads to worry. Think and meditate on God, His presence, and on His person. As you do that, you are cultivating His presence in your life. Put this into practice.

CHAPTER TWELVE

HONORING THE PRESENCE OF GOD

Honor is one of the greatest missing ingredients in the Lord's house today. In 1 Samuel 2:30, the Bible teaches us that God will honor those who honor Him and despise those who despise Him.

> Therefore the LORD, the God of Israel, declares: 'I promised that members of your family would minister before me forever.' But now the LORD declares: 'Far be it from me! Those who honor me I will honor, but those who despise me will be disdained. (1 Samuel 2:30, NIV)

One of the reasons why we do not see revivals in our personal lives is because of the culture of dishonor that has permeated the church. We have dishonored the Lord, His Word, His presence, His ministers, and His calling. One may ask, how do we honor God? For a better understanding, let's look at the difference between honor and dishonor before we answer this question.

WHAT IS DISHONOR?

Dishonor means to treat someone with disrespect, irreverence, profanity as if worthless or common. Dishonor will block God's power and bring about disfavor in our lives.

WHAT IS HONOR?

Honor is a show of reverence that comes from the heart. It is deep respect and admiration that causes us to hold something in high esteem. Honor causes us to value something, look at it as special, and treat it with absolute respect. The Bible shows us the manifest presence of God deserves honor:

> And he said, Draw not nigh hither: put off thy shoes from off thy feet, for the place whereon thou standest is holy ground. Moreover he said, I am the God of thy father, the God of Abraham, the God of Isaac, and the God of Jacob. And Moses hid his face; for he was afraid to look upon God. (Exodus 3:5–6)

The manifest presence of God deserves reverence and honor as evidenced in the above scriptures when God asked Moses to take off his sandals from his feet. Generally, in ancient times, before the time of Moses, Egyptians and Orientals removed their sandals (or their shoes) from their feet before entering any place to which respect was due: temple, palace, and even the private house of a great man. It is important to note God Himself orders this mark of respect to be shown to the place where His presence is. God's presence must and should be honored, not taken lightly. His presence must be hallowed and reverenced!

As we deal with this subject of honoring the presence of God, it is my prayer this teaching takes you to a place of awareness where His presence means everything to you. God's presence should mean more than food, friends, schooling, or your job. Embracing and honoring the presence of God brings everything you need into your life.

We established earlier in Exodus 33:15–16 that the presence of God makes the distinction between a believer and a nonbeliever. So it is important that we know how to honor God's presence to experience continuous manifestation of His glory in and upon our lives. Moses said unto God:

> If Your presence does not go with us, do not bring us up from here. For how then will it be known that Your people and I have found grace in Your sight, except You go with us? So we shall be separate, Your people and I, from all the people who are upon the face of the earth. (Exodus 33:15–16, NKJV)

In this scripture, Moses is honoring the presence of God by putting a very high premium on it. Moses is holding God's presence in very high esteem by basically saying to God, "God, if your presence is not going to be manifesting in our lives then we don't want to go on this journey."

Honoring God's presence starts with our devotion time. We need to set aside time for thanksgiving, praise, and worship of the Father (prayer). Spending time in His presence must have first priority in our lives. As you honor His presence in private, His anointing. Honor His voice.

We also honor God's presence through our words and service to Him. It is very important that we put it first in our lives, as well as welcome and meditate on it continually. The respect you place on somebody shows the honor you have for them.

Honoring the presence of God refers to respecting God's presence on your life, the lives of other people who carry His presence or in a corporate setting. How much honor or respect do you have for the presence of God? It is so humbling to know the presence of God is the most precious personality in eternity; yet, God Himself decided to tabernacle in us and dwell among us.

It is important to know those you honor are more likely to spend time with you. Those you dishonor will not want to make their presence known to you. People will go where they are accepted and celebrated, not where they are simply tolerated or rejected. So, as you honor God's presence, you are creating an atmosphere of it around you.

So many Christians miss out on the very presence of God by not honoring His presence. Therefore, they miss out on God working in their lives. God wants you to honor His presence in your life and in the lives of others, even corporately.

Remember, to honor is to hold in high esteem; to have high respect for. You honor God's presence by putting high esteem on it. To honor the Holy Spirit's presence means to highly respect the presence of God and let it mean more than life to you. No wonder a song writer once wrote, "Your presence is heaven to me."

Honoring God's presence is making it a priority in your existence in such a way that it means more to you than anything in your life. As God's child, He wants you to honor His presence. The more you honor His presence, the more it manifests in your life and the more you change the atmosphere you are in.

Continually honoring the Holy Spirit's presence in your life brings breakthroughs and sets you free from any kind of bondage. Honoring the Holy Spirit's presence should not be optional; you should intentionally be living by the Holy Spirit and honoring Him at all times. When you honor Him, you camp around His presence; you think about His presence. When you wake up in the morning, you look forward to experiencing the move of the Holy Spirit upon your life, because His presence really means a lot to you.

As born-again believers, we have the Holy Spirit living in us because we were sealed with Him unto the day of redemption. However, God says we should not grieve Him. Rather, we ought to respect and honor Him. It is important to know the extent to which the Holy Spirit manifests His presence in you is dependent on you.

Jesus promised the Holy Spirit will live in you and it happens the moment you give your life to Him. However, the manifestation of His presence upon your life is totally dependent upon you. You determine how much of God's presence is released in your life. Honoring or dishonoring the Holy Spirit determines the extent to which His presence is manifested upon you. Let's see what the Bible says in Ephesians 4:29–30 about honoring the presence of God,

> Let no corrupt word proceed out of your mouth, but what is good for necessary edification, that it may impart grace to the hearers. And do not grieve the Holy Spirit of God, by whom you were sealed for the day of redemption. (Ephesians 4:29–30, NKJV)

From the scripture, we see you honor the presence of God by not grieving the Holy Spirit. One may ask, how can a person grieve the Holy Spirit? The following scripture tells us how not to grieve the Holy Spirit:

> Let all bitterness, wrath, anger, clamor, and evil speaking be put away from you, with all malice. (Ephesians 4:31, NKJV)

You grieve the Holy Spirit through your words. In John 6:63b, Jesus said, "The words that I speak to you are spirit and they are life." When you honor people, you do it intentionally, not by coincidence. When you honor the people in your life, you respect them. Similarly, the honor of the Holy Spirit should be more intentional than coincidental. Highly esteeming the people you respect brings honor and whosoever you honor has a desire to be in your presence.

So, you might be asking yourself, "How can I honor the Holy Spirit?"

To answer that question, let's see what the Bible tells us about not grieving the Holy Spirit. Ephesians 4:29–31 says not to allow corrupt communication or foul words to come out of our mouths. The Spirit of God in you can be dishonored by foul communication, bitterness, losing your temper, wrath, anger, clamor, slander, evil speaking, and malice. These things dishonor His presence. God wants you to honor His presence through your words, attitude, and in your heart toward others. In James 1:20, the Bible says, "The wrath of man worketh not the righteousness of God."

Intentionally honor the Holy Spirit's presence in your life by watching the words you speak, because words are spirits. When you release those words, bear in mind, they are either honoring or dishonoring the presence of God in your life. When you watch the words you say, your honor for the presence of God will no longer be coincidental. Be deliberate about this and make up your mind to honor the Holy Spirit and not quench His move in your life. Oftentimes, Christians quench or grieve the Holy Spirit without knowing it. For something to be quenched it must initially be on flaming fire; pouring water on it would extinguish the fire or put it out. Similarly, the move of the Holy Spirit in your life can be quenched by the words that you speak, your attitude, or your heart toward others.

When you allow corrupt communication or foul words to come out of your mouth, you quench the Holy Spirit. When you quench the Holy Spirit, you are also dishonoring His presence. The Holy Spirit is honored when you watch what you say to ensure it lines up with the Word of God.

The more you quench the presence of God in your life, the more you exhibit dishonor of His presence. God wants us to have the mindset to honor His presence. When you honor His presence, not only in your life, but in the lives of others and in a corporate setting, you give Him a reason to be excited about you. Some people do not give the Holy Spirit precedence in their lives or time of worship, but as God's people, we must make up our minds and be intentional about honoring His presence.

Let us look at what happened in John 12:1–8, where the Bible talks about how Mary poured very precious, costly oil on the feet of Jesus and wiped them with her hair causing the house to be filled with fragrance from the oil. That was an example of honoring the presence of God.

> Then, six days before the Passover, Jesus came to
> Bethany, where Lazarus was who had been dead, whom
> He had raised from the dead. There they made Him

a supper; and Martha served, but Lazarus was one of those who sat at the table with Him. Then Mary took a pound of very costly oil of spikenard, anointed the feet of Jesus, and wiped His feet with her hair. And the house was filled with the fragrance of the oil. But one of His disciples, Judas Iscariot, Simon's son, who would betray Him, said, "Why was this fragrant oil not sold for three hundred denarii and given to the poor?" This he said, not that he cared for the poor, but because he was a thief, and had the money box; and he used to take what was put in it. But Jesus said, "Let her alone; she has kept this for the day of My burial. For the poor you have with you always, but Me you do not have always." (John 12:1–8, NKJV)

The Holy Spirit is also honored when you look forward to worshiping in His presence and when you sacrifice things that mean a lot to you. Mary worshipped Jesus and sacrificed the precious oil for Him.

When you speak positively about the Holy Spirit and His presence, it means a lot to Him. It also means a lot to the Holy Spirit when you refuse to grieve or quench His presence. God wants us to honor His presence by talking about it positively, by worshiping Him in His presence, by giving in His presence, by not grieving Him with our words, and not having bad attitudes toward other people. Honoring God's presence should be deliberate.

I challenge you to continually honor the presence of God, because whosoever you honor manifests themselves to you. Whosoever you respect will make their presence known to you at all times. Why don't you just make up your mind right now to have great respect and high esteem for the presence of God? Make up your mind to think about His presence day and night and let Him know how much you love His presence. Just say, "Dear Jesus, I honor Your presence." Let Him know how much His presence means to you in your life. Let Him know how much your life is changing because of His presence. When you chase after God, it shows you are honoring Him.

I believe as you start to live your life like this, you will begin to experience the peace, joy, and tranquility His presence brings. When you honor others, they release all of themselves to you. So as you honor the Holy Spirit's presence in your life, you experience greater dimensions of the work of God.

I know many of you reading this book would like to operate in the power of God and move in the anointing of the Holy Spirit. So, let me give you the secret to this. Honor His presence! Even as you lay on your bed, honor His presence; be aware His presence is always with you. Remember whatever you say and your attitude toward others will dishonor or honor the presence of the Holy Spirit. It is my prayer His presence will be very evident and so real in your life that wherever you go, it will not only be seen upon you, but it will also be manifested through you because you are honoring the person and the presence of the Holy Spirit.

CHAPTER THIRTEEN

CELEBRATING THE PRESENCE OF GOD

———

The presence of God is so great and amazing it is worth celebrating. To celebrate is to acknowledge something or someone with a happy and joyful activity. When somebody is celebrating, he or she is happy, excited, and very joyful about the particular situation being celebrated. As we individually and corporately celebrate God's presence in our lives, we experience more of His manifest presence, His blessings, and provisions. We always go to where we are celebrated and not just tolerated. You must learn how to celebrate God's presence because, as you do so, you will experience an abundance of His manifest presence in your life.

David knew how to celebrate God's presence; we see that in 2 Samuel 6:12. When you read the preceding verses they tell us what caused the Ark of the Covenant to be carried into the house of Obed-edom. David became afraid of the Lord because His wrath had broken out against Uzzah, who got struck dead because of his irreverent act of touching the Ark of the Lord. For that reason, David was no longer willing to take the

Ark to be with him in the city of David. Instead, he took it to the house of Obed-Edom, where it remained for three months.

> Then King David was told, "The Lord has blessed Obed-edom's household and everything he has because of the Ark of God." So David went there and brought the Ark of God from the house of Obed-edom to the City of David with a great celebration. (2 Samuel 6:12, NLT)

From this scripture, we see how God blessed Obed-edom and his entire household tremendously during the time the Ark was in his house. The Ark of the Covenant represented the presence of God, and we see in the above scripture how David and God's people celebrated the presence of God. Wherever God's presence is, there is blessing, provision, joy, pleasure, and peace. As you celebrate God's presence, all these things manifest in your life. You have to understand that whatsoever you celebrate manifests greatly in your life. When you celebrate people, they want to be around you all the time, but if you act as if you are tolerating them, they want to get out of your presence.

David celebrated the presence of God because it had been brought back to the city of David. As a child of God, you must celebrate the presence of God every day by talking about it and acknowledging it with a joyful heart and mindset. You must be happy about God's presence because, in His presence, there is fullness of joy. His presence is your very means of existence. Without His presence in your life, your life is sunk and in big trouble. You must celebrate God's presence. The more you celebrate God's presence, the more it is evident in your life. That means that the radiance of God's glory becomes so real because you are celebrating God's presence that is upon your life, in the life of others, and also in the corporate setting.

> You will show me the way of life, granting me the joy of your presence and the pleasures of living with you forever. (Psalm 16:11, NLT)

This scripture tells us there is joy in God's presence. When you celebrate God's presence, there is a countenance of joy. His presence grants you joy, and you remain joyful. Being joyful is an indication of God's presence. You should make celebrating God's presence your lifestyle.

There are people who believe the presence of God should be more of a reverence or something to be feared, which is wonderful. We must reverence the presence of God, but there is nothing in the Bible that tells us in reverencing God's presence, we don't have to celebrate it. We must celebrate Him with joy, exuberance, and happiness. When you wake up in the morning, you must celebrate His presence with joy in your heart. As you lay on the bed, celebrate His presence with joy in your heart. With that joyful attitude and disposition toward His presence, you are celebrating it.

Celebrate God; always talk about Him. In everything you do, let there be a sign God's presence is celebrated on your life. When you know how to celebrate God's presence, you will start experiencing His tangible presence in your life all the time. It is important to understand how to celebrate God's presence because whatever you celebrate you attract. Whatever you celebrate manifests in a greater dimension in your life.

WHAT CELEBRATING GOD'S PRESENCE ENTAILS

You may be asking yourself, what does celebrating God's presence really entail? To answer this question, let's look at 2 Samuel 6:13–15, in which we find four elements about celebrating the presence of God:

1. Sacrifice
2. Dancing
3. Shouting
4. Singing

Let's take a closer look at these four elements:

1. Sacrifice
   Celebrating God's presence requires sacrifice.

   > After the men who were carrying the Ark of the LORD
   > had gone six steps, <u>David sacrificed a bull and a fattened
   > calf</u>. (2 Samuel 6:13, NLT)

   Giving unto the Lord in His presence is a form of sacrifice and a
   great opportunity we should always tap into when it presents itself.
   When you are celebrating God's presence, it is not complete without
   sacrifice. Giving your time and talent to the things of the Lord is
   a form of sacrifice. In the house of God, there is a consciousness of
   His presence, so celebrate it by giving offerings to God. Before you
   go to the house of the Lord, prepare to meet and celebrate the King
   of kings and Lord of lords with all your heart by giving from the
   abundance He has blessed you with. The Bible tells us in Exodus
   23:15 that no one shall appear before God emptyhanded.

   > Celebrate the Festival of Unleavened Bread; for seven
   > days eat bread made without yeast, as I commanded
   > you. Do this at the appointed time in the month of Aviv,
   > for in that month you came out of Egypt. <u>No one is to
   > appear before me empty-handed</u>. (Exodus 23:15, NIV)

   It is important you understand that celebrating God's presence
   brings about a greater manifestation of it in your life. The more
   you develop a mindset of celebrating God, the more God's manifest
   presence will be evident in you. Always give to the Lord the sacrifice
   of your time, talent, and resources because when you sacrifice in His
   presence, you are celebrating Him.

2. Dancing
   Dancing before God's presence is a way of celebrating it.

And <u>David danced before the Lord with all his might</u>, wearing a priestly garment. So David and all the people of Israel brought up the Ark of the Lord with shouts of joy and the blowing of rams' horns. (2 Samuel 6:14–15, NLT)

In this scripture, we see David celebrated God's presence by dancing before the Lord with all his might. When was the last time you celebrated God's presence in your life through dancing? When was the last time you danced in your home, car, kitchen, living room, or bathroom because of God's presence? The more you celebrate God's presence with dance, the more His presence becomes prevalent in your life. God wants you and me to celebrate His presence through dancing as David did with all his might. Consider dancing before the Lord.

Praise his name with dancing, accompanied by tambourine and harp. (Psalm 149:3, NLT)

David danced before the Lord with his priestly garment and was not ashamed as a priest; no wonder the Bible says in Acts 13:22, David was a man after God's own heart.

In 1 Peter 2:9, the Bible says you are a royal priesthood, so you are permitted to dance before the Lord as David did. Dance because you know His presence is with you. Dance because you know His presence is manifesting in your life. It may sound very unreal, but it is scriptural that celebrating the Lord involves dancing before Him. As a Christian, it is important to dance before the Lord and celebrate His presence.

3. Shouting
Some people believe when you come to the presence of the Lord you have to remain quiet and still. That is wonderful, but it is not always the case. The presence of the Lord is also a place of shouting. We see that in Scripture:

> So David and all the people of Israel brought up the Ark
> of the LORD <u>with shouts of joy</u> and the blowing of rams'
> horns. (2 Samuel 6:15, NLT)

David and all the people of Israel were so excited about the presence of the Lord, they celebrated it with shouts of joy and the blowing of ram's horns. It is okay to be quiet in God's presence when you have to hear from Him, but that does not mean you must always be quiet. We see in the above scripture that the presence of the Lord can be celebrated with shouting. So the presence of the Lord is not only a place of quietness and stillness, but it can also be a place of shouting before the Lord. When you are celebrating God's presence, you must have a shout of joy; that is why we do that quite often in the House of the Lord at Spirit Temple Bible Church (STBC). A joyful shout unto the Lord is a way of celebrating His presence.

> Come, everyone! Clap your hands! <u>Shout to God with
> joyful praise</u>! (Psalm 47:1, NLT)

Celebrate the presence of God in your life by making a joyful shout unto Him. Learn to shout exuberantly in celebration of God's presence. Shout unto the Lord with a voice of triumph; shout unto the Lord with the voice of praise. As you do this, you are celebrating the Lord. The more you celebrate God the more He manifests in your life.

4. Singing

    We can also celebrate God's presence with singing. Yes, there is no celebration without singing. When you begin to celebrate God's presence with singing, it makes a great difference. God wants His presence to manifest in your life and for it to be so real to you. As you begin to celebrate God's presence, it does not only start to manifest in your life, but it also becomes so real and tangible you literally carry it upon you wherever you go. This happens when you celebrate God's presence so much with singing that it gets to be upon your life. We see this in the book of Zephaniah:

> For the LORD your God is living among you. He is a
> mighty savior. He will take delight in you with gladness.
> With his love, he will calm all your fears. <u>He will rejoice
> over you with joyful songs</u>." (Zephaniah 3:17, NLT)

Let us now look at the same scripture in the King James Version,

> The LORD thy God in the midst of thee is mighty; he
> will save, he will rejoice over thee with joy; he will rest in
> his love, <u>he will joy over thee with singing</u>. (Zephaniah
> 3:17)

This scripture tells us God Himself celebrates you as His child with
singing. The same way God celebrates you with singing, you should
also celebrate and rejoice over Him with singing. What a way to
celebrate God! As you rejoice over the Lord with singing the way He
rejoices over you, great things happen in your life.

As you apply these simple, yet profound nuggets about celebrating
God's presence, you will see more manifestations of it in your life.
God wants you to experience Him in a greater dimension. He wants
you to carry His presence everywhere you go; He wants to see His
presence manifest everywhere you go. He wants you to allow His
presence to just permeate every area of your life. Let His presence
be evident in your living room, bedroom, car, kitchen, everywhere
you go.

Let your pictures in the house remind you of His presence. Let the
artwork in your bedroom remind you of His presence. Let your Bible
be placed where it reminds you of His presence. Let everything you
do remind you of His presence. Continue to celebrate His presence
because the more you celebrate the presence of God, the more His
presence is manifested in your life. You must have a heart to celebrate
the Lord as you engage these principles.

Continue celebrating God's presence in your life. As you do, you will experience more of His manifest presence and your life will never remain the same again. This is because God's presence is more precious than anything you will ever desire.

I challenge you to practice celebrating the presence of God through these four principles I have shared with you. Put them into practice because whatever you have learned will only do you good if it is acted upon. Follow these principles and see God's manifest presence become real in your life.

CHAPTER FOURTEEN

MAKING ROOM FOR THE PRESENCE OF GOD

Making room for the presence of God refers to putting God in a high place in your life. Whatever you make room for takes a bigger place in your life. When you make room for God's presence, it takes greater precedence in your life. The more time or room, you give to the presence of God, the more evident His manifest presence will be in your life. From what we have already discussed, we understand God's presence is more precious than life itself. As God's people, we must not only have a desire for His presence, but we also have to make room for it. If you do not make room for somebody in your life, the person will not feel welcomed. You must not allow the distractions of life to take you away from making room for the presence of God. His presence is more than all you will ever need in your life. Yes, God's presence is not comparable to anything you can ever desire.

Unfortunately, we have lost the art of God's presence in our generation, but we must bring it back into its rightful place. God's presence is more important than sitting around a sermon. In the wilderness, the Israelites sat around His presence which guided them, led them, and directed them everywhere they went. Moses said to God, "If Your presence will not go with us then do not take us there." That should be the heart's desire of every child of God. "If Your presence will not go with us to this location don't take us there."

We have to make room for God's presence in our lives. We must change our schedules to accommodate His presence. For instance, assume I come to visit you in your home, and you not only change your schedule to accommodate my presence in your home, but you also make room for me and make me feel welcomed. This would send a great message to me and make me feel very comfortable and welcomed. I would therefore make myself comfortable in your home because you made room for me. This is the same for God's presence. When you make room for the manifest presence of God, it leads to a greater manifestation of God's glory in your life.

Many of us desire and seek the radiance, the glory, and the power of God in our lives. However, what we may not know is that the extent to which we create room for His presence is the same extent to which His presence will manifest in our lives. If you want God's glory to be tangible in you, you must start making room and time for His presence.

God really wants to do great things in and through you. In Zechariah 4:6b, the Bible says, it is "not by might or power but by my spirit saith the Lord." Making room for God's presence should be your greatest inspiration as a child of God because it is by His presence that miracles happen.

Beyond being born again, God's presence is the next glorious thing in our lives. It is important you understand this and start making room for God's presence in your life. When you make room for God's manifest presence, it leads to greater manifestation of His glory upon you. Hence, the 2 Corinthians 3:18 says as we behold His glory with our open faces, we become transformed into the very glory of God and we go from glory to glory.

> But we all, with open face <u>beholding</u> as in a glass <u>the glory of the Lord</u>, are changed into the same image from glory to glory, even as by the Spirit of the Lord. (2 Corinthians 3:18)

This scripture says, "beholding the glory of the Lord," which means making room and taking time to contemplate and to meditate on His presence. Oftentimes, our lives are crowded with so many issues that prevent us from making room for the manifestation of God's presence in our lives. An example would be our jobs, businesses, and families just to name a few. That's why it must be a deliberate action, and an intentional move, for you to make room for God's presence in your life. It will not just happen automatically.

God's presence manifesting in your life is vital to your very existence. We can only thrive and succeed in our supernatural walk with God to the extent to which we make room for His presence in our lives. Remember, God's desire for you is that you manifest His presence all the days of your life. You must be intentional about making room for His presence. I understand we live in a fast-paced world, always busy and productive, but making room for God's presence in our lives must be a priority as this is the key to a successful supernatural living. The only way you can really experience victory and supernatural manifestation is when you make room for God's presence in your life. Don't allow the events of life, circumstances and issues of life to consume your time so much you forget to create room for the manifestation of God's presence. Be intentional about doing it.

> They brought the Ark of the LORD and set it in its place inside the special tent David had prepared for it. And David sacrificed burnt offerings and peace offerings to the LORD. (2 Samuel 6:17, NLT)

In this scripture, we can see David was intentional about making room for the presence of the Lord by building a special tent to house the Ark of the presence of God. We are the temples of the living God. In as much as we worship God in our places of worship, and experience His presence in the house of the Lord, we must be aware we are the tabernacles not made with human hands, where God resides. He has made us carriers of His presence. The practical application of what David did would be to make room in our lives for God's presence to practice it. We also have to make time in our lives to experience, live in, and walk in His manifest presence.

> Come close to God, and God will come close to you.
> (James 4:8a, NLT)

In this scripture, we see we have a responsibility to make room in our lives to draw near to God. It doesn't happen automatically. You must set up time in your life to do so. When you draw near to God, God draws near to you. Drawing near to God cannot happen by coincidence; we have to be intentional about it. The more we draw near to God, the more we experience His manifest presence. Let everything in your life revolve around God. This means to put God first in your very existence and let Him be the center of your life. Let God come before your job, family, and everything in your life. The only way God's presence can be real in your life is when you make room for Him. Call unto God and draw near to Him, and He will draw near to you.

> The LORD is near to all who call upon Him,
> To all who call upon Him in truth. (Psalm 145:18, NASB)

This scripture tells us what happens when we draw near to God by calling upon Him and making room for Him. He draws near to us and makes His presence known to us. So as you call upon the Lord, His presence becomes evident in your life. Life without God's presence is very dry and empty. Don't allow anyone or anything to stop you from creating room for God's presence. The greatest experience you can ever have in life is manifesting God's presence in your life.

To intentionally make room for the presence of God in your life you must:

1. Have heartfelt worship
2. Have a time of meditating on His Word
3. Begin to ask God to increase your hunger for His presence
4. Engage in intimate prayer

Let's take an in-depth look at each of these:

1. Have Heartfelt Worship

   To make room for the presence of God in your life, you must be intentional about making heartfelt worship a major part of your life. It is imperative you make room for a moment of worship each day, whether it is in a corporate or church setting; worship needs to be a major part of your life. The worship becomes heartfelt when we focus on the Lord, not on ourselves or our circumstances during worship. When you focus on your problems and circumstances then the worship is about you.

   I have been to many church services around the world and noticed contemporary Christian music playing and the people drawing attention to themselves, not God. When you want to make room for God and experience His presence, there must be heartfelt worship targeted to God, not to yourself. Worship is not for us to be hyped up in our souls or bodies; it is for our spirits to be connected to God. When our spirits are connected to God, His presence is released in a mighty way in our midst. Every Christian worship leader should focus the worship on God, not men, as worship is all about giving God His due respect.

   Would you like to experience an increase in God's manifest presence in your life? If so, I challenge you to make worshiping God a routine of your personal devotion time. Making room for the Lord's presence through worship during our time of personal devotion increases our level of expectation of God's presence. To really see the manifest presence of God, we must engage in deep heartfelt worship with expectant hearts.

It is when you expect God's presence that it begins to manifest in your life. When you make room for God through heartfelt worship, it also creates a spirit of expectancy, and expectancy is a breeding ground for miracles. God's presence can become so real in your life when you expect Him to show up. When we expect God, He releases Himself in our midst and personal lives.

It is important to create a place of worship in your home, a place you go to every time to meet with God. There may be nothing special about that place, but it is a time of significance, which you set apart to go to the Lord and worship Him. When you do that, you make room for the Lord in your heart.

Why do you go to church every Sunday? It is because the church is a place of worship where room has been made for us to go and have an encounter with God. So every time you worship God and expect to have an encounter, you are making room for Him. God wants you to make room for Him, so you can have an encounter with Him. Yes, an encounter with the King of kings and Lord of lords, an encounter with the presence of the Almighty God. This encounter comes from having heartfelt worship and an expectation to experience and encounter the presence of God. Make time to worship God with an expectant heart because your expectation of God's presence makes room for it to manifest in your life.

2. Have Time of Meditating on God's Word
   Making room for God's presence is equivalent to making room and time, to absorb, and think on His Word. You cannot say you are making room for God's presence in your life when there is no time of studying, meditating, and absorbing His Word into your spirit.

   > This book of the law shall not depart from your mouth,
   > but you shall meditate on it day and night, so that you
   > may be careful to do according to all that is written in it;

for then you will make your way prosperous, and then you will have success. (Joshua 1:8, NASB)

This scripture is talking about meditating on God's Word. When you meditate on God's Word, it is an indication of making room for His presence in your life. Meditating on God's Word results in it being absorbed into your spirit. This creates an atmosphere of His manifest presence in your life. The more you meditate on God's Word, the more the glory of the Word of God transforms you into the very image of the glory you are beholding and an ever-increasing glory. We find this in 2 Corinthians 3:18, which shows us the importance of making room for the presence of God by meditating on His Word.

But we all, with open face beholding as in a glass the glory of the Lord, are changed into the same image from glory to glory, even as by the Spirit of the Lord. (2 Corinthians 3:18)

You must make room for meditating on the Word of God. It doesn't just happen; it is an intentional act. Make time to get into God's Word every day.

3. Ask God for an Increase of Hunger for His Presence
   You have to ask God to put a hunger for His presence in your heart. When you do so, that indicates you are making room for His manifest presence in your life and God puts a hunger for His presence in your heart. When you ask God to put more hunger in your heart for His presence, it indicates you are making more room for His manifest presence in your life. You will eventually experience more hunger for His presence. When you continuously desire His presence in your life, He puts the hunger there and it becomes a continuous cycle of seeking Him and making room for His presence. God continuously gives you more hunger as you desire more.

Blessed are they which do hunger and thirst after righteousness: for they shall be filled. (Matthew 5:6)

As you make room for more of God's presence, you get hungry for His Word. This scripture tells us that you will be filled because it is God who placed that hunger in your heart.

4. Engage in Intimate Prayer

Making room for God's presence is opening up for an intimate time of prayer, a time when you converse with God and listen to His response. I know you may just try to talk to God when you need something from Him, but when you really want to experience His presence, intimate prayer time is not a place for making demands or having a laundry list of what you want God to do for you. It is a place of intimate one-on-one communication with God when you converse with Him and listen for His response. When you do that, you are creating room for Him to respond to you; hence, you make room for His presence.

But be filled with the Spirit. (Ephesians 5:18b)

We have an active part to play in making room for the Lord's manifest presence in our lives. Every day, I intentionally make room for God's presence to manifest in my life; it does not just happen. If you want to see God's presence manifesting in your life, you must make room for it. God's presence manifests greatly in STBC worldwide because, a group of people make room for it so we can see God's manifestation in our services and lives.

You cannot carry God's presence upon your life if you have not spent time in it. If you want to have God's presence, then spend time in His presence. When you spend time in somebody's presence, it comes upon you.

So, for God's presence to be upon your life, you need to be intentional about spending time with Him and making heartfelt worship a major part of your life. You need to create time to meditate on His Word, ask God to increase your hunger for His presence, and engage in an intimate time of prayer with God.

I truly pray you have been blessed by reading this book. I also pray your desire for more of God's presence in your life increases as a result of the teaching in this book. God bless you. And remember making room for the presence of God requires your active participation. You must make a deliberate decision to do so for God's manifest presence to be evident in your life.

CONCLUSION

What do you want to do with this information you've received? If you have not yet accepted the free gift of forgiveness and eternal life Jesus offers, you cannot experience the presence of God that was talked about in this book. You can accept that free gift right now by repeating this simple prayer:

Dear Father, I come to You right now as a person who needs Jesus in my life. Thank You, Jesus, for dying for all my sins. I accept the free gift of forgiveness and eternal life You offer. I confess with my mouth Jesus is Lord, and I believe in my heart He rose from the dead. Dear Jesus, come into my heart. Be my Lord and Savior. In Jesus' name. Amen.

If you have said this simple prayer, the Bible says you are born again and on your way to live your best life ever (Romans 10:9–10).

The presence of God is for you to experience and live out of. Desire it, go for it, and walk in the presence and anointing of the Holy Ghost.

ABOUT THE AUTHOR

Dr. Ese Duke is the founder and the general overseer of Spirit Temple Bible Church. He is the president of Spiritual Father Apostolic Covering where he provides spiritual and ministerial covering to leaders, ministries and churches across the globe. He is also the founder, president, and rector of Spirit Temple Bible College with Headquarters based in Bethlehem, PA.USA.

He is a man after God's heart, a dynamic preacher and teacher of God's Word with an apostolic calling. He has made tremendous impact in the lives of people all across the world bringing the message of God's amazing love, grace, healing, and prosperity with a mandate from God according to Isaiah 61:1–2.

His ministry is characterized by the teaching of the awesome revelation of God's Word in simplicity and clarity, the move of God's power with tangible proofs of healing, miracles, signs, wonders, accurate word of knowledge and manifestations of prophetic declaration.

He is happily married to Reverend Gladys Duke, a co-laborer in the ministry and God's vineyard. They are blessed with six lovely and God-honoring children.

Also Available

The Anointing:
The Supernatural Power of God
Apostle Ese Duke

In *The Anointing*, author Apostle Ese Duke offers a reverential look at the anointing of the Holy Spirit, the supernatural power of God that gives believers the ability to fulfil their God-given purpose. Apostle Ese Duke discusses:

- what the anointing is
- how to prepare to receive the anointing
- the levels and dimensions of the anointing
- the laws operating the anointing
- the difference between the anointing within and the anointing upon
- how the anointing functions and grows
- how to release the anointing
- how to keep the anointing flowing and many more impactful, life-changing teachings

The Anointing presents a look at God's power working in an ordinary man to bring about the supernatural in the lives and affairs of men.

A copy of this book can be obtained at:
https://esedukeministry.org/product/the-anointing-the-supernatural-power-of-god/

Hardcover: 9781480870321   Softcover: 9781480870314   E-Book: 9781480870338